THE OFFICIAL
JAMES BOND 007
MOVIE BOOK

007™

007

THE OFFICIAL JAMES BOND 007 MOVIE BOOK

Sally Hibbin

Foreword by

ALBERT R. BROCCOLI

Crown Publishers, Inc.
New York

Published in the United States by Crown Publishers, Inc.,
225 Park Avenue South, New York, New York 10003
and represented in Canada by the Canadian MANDA Group.
Published in Great Britain by The Hamlyn Publishing Group Ltd.,
Bridge House, 69 London Road, Twickenham, Middlesex TW1 3SB.
CROWN is a trademark of Crown Publishers, Inc.

Manufactured in Italy.

Library of Congress Cataloging in Publication Data
Hibbin, Sally.
The official James Bond 007 movie book.
1. James Bond films – History and criticism.
I. Title
PN1995.9.J3H5   1987   791.43'09'09351   87-5057
ISBN 0-517-56643-5
10 9 8 7 6 5 4 3 2 1
First Edition

This book deals with the 25 years of James Bond 007 films, from *Dr No* onwards, made by Eon
Productions Ltd. It does not include *Casino Royale* or *Never Say Never Again* which were not made
by Eon.

Acknowledgments
Many photographers covered the Bond sets over the years. To pay them tribute we mention the
following few: Graham Attwood, Bert Cann, Albert Clarke, Frank Connor, Arthur Evans, Keith
Hamshere, Ray Hearne, David James, Peter Kernot, Patrick Morin, Joe Pearce, Bob Penn, James
Juroe, Derek Coyte and Meg Grimes at Eon Productions and John Parkinson at Glidrose
Publications. The Publishers also thank Warner Home Video for their cooperation.
The Publishers gratefully acknowledge the indefatigable and invaluable assistance of Charles
and Linda Swarbrick and George Whitear.
It is impossible in a book of this size to mention by name everyone who has made a creative
contribution to the James Bond 007 films, but this book is a testament to skills and talents of all
the actors, production personnel and others who have worked on the series over the last quarter
of a century. The publishers apologize for any unintentional errors or omissions.
The listing of names in the dossiers is not necessarily based on contractual obligations.

CONTENTS

FOREWORD

This book marks the twenty-fifth anniversary of the first James Bond movie. 007 had to find a place on celluloid: Fleming's stories were made to be turned into films and over the years I am proud to have been involved with fifteen Bonds which are among the most successful British films of all time.

With Timothy Dalton, we enter a new era of our series. There are many terrific young actors about but it is hard to cast 007. Sean Connery was the original – and, therefore, the model; Roger Moore made Bond his own in a different way, adding a little more humour. Timothy Dalton is a remarkably fine actor and with him we are ready for another suave and dynamic hero to emerge and entertain us.

Although the actors playing the leading role have changed, the action, the humour, the exotic locations and the beautiful women are the stamp of a James Bond 007 film and that will always remain. From the very first, I knew that Bond was forever and I have enjoyed working on it over the years with our actors, technicians and the support of the people at Pinewood Studios and United Artists. Without them the series would never have been made and I see myself continuing as long as I can move around.

Browsing through this book has brought back many happy memories over the years. I am convinced that every Bond fan will derive as much enjoyment from it as I have done.

THE BOND MOVIE PHENOMENON

The background story to the most successful film series of all time.

For 25 years, the James Bond 007 film series, produced by Eon Productions, has entertained cinema audiences around the world with its unique blend of action, glamour, technology and humour. From *Dr No* to *The Living Daylights*, the fifteenth in the series, the films have gone from strength to strength at the box-office as people flock to see the latest adventure. The Fleming fans, who eagerly devoured each new novel as it was published, have been joined by younger cinemagoers, won to Bond through the films themselves. And the audiences have stayed loyal, greeting each new Bond movie with delight to see how, once again, 007 saves Western civilization from destruction.

Over the years of the series' existence, there have been a staggering 1.75 billion paid admissions to see the films. In addition, with chart-topping TV showings and video sales, it is estimated that over half the world's population has seen a Bond movie.

During those 25 years, the series has never rested on its laurels. It has continually sought out new talent, new exotic locations, new breath-taking stunts and new up-to-the-minute imaginative gimmicks. It has kept abreast of the times, transforming Fleming's sometimes dated hero into a man of the Eighties, coping with high-tech and space-age adventure. Its women, too, have changed, from the beautiful but precious girls of the early Bonds to their more active and competent (though still beautiful) heirs in tune with the aspirations of the modern woman. At the same time, its humour has moved with the mood of the audience, from irony to self-mockery, to key into cinematic trends of the times.

But while much has changed, much has also stayed the same giving the series a coherence across its duration. Bond, with his precise cocktail instructions, his penchant for attractive women and fast cars, his ability to tell a true Englishman by his choice of wines, his fast-thinking in tight situations and his willingness to use his fists or the famous Walther PPK when all else fails, has retained his endearing characteristics through four changes of actor. The nuances, from Connery's brutal charm to Moore's more sophisticated ease, may have shifted but the essential Bond has remained. Now, Timothy Dalton makes his own mark on the character with his first appearance as 007 in *The Living Daylights*.

The Secret Service background has also helped to give the series a continuity from film to film. However much M has a tendency to pop up in remote corners, his office in London with its panelled walls and double doors is always there. And M himself, never quite sure if he values Bond's encyclopedic knowledge or despises his upper-class pedantry, carries on as the Head of the Secret Service, maintaining his tetchy relationship with 007. Miss Moneypenny, his secretary, with her constant, hopeless flirtation with Bond, remains calmly efficient. This guardian of the outer office is always on the ball owing to her deft use of the departmental intercom. On the other hand, the gruffly lovable Q, the head of the Service's weapons branch, with his fondness for experimental gadgets and hatred of Bond's disregard for government

Author Ian Fleming, a visitor to the location filming of From Russia With Love, *poses for the stills photographer in front of the engine of the Orient Express.*

using all the elements that audiences have come to know and love – the erotic, glowing main titles, the spectacular ski, car and boat chases, the beautiful underwater scenes, the pacy sound-tracks in which the 'James Bond theme' plays a major part, the up-to-the moment title song rendered by a popular artist, the fantastic sets and well-crafted explosions which often end the films, the endless seductions as each new woman falls for Bond's charm, the aerial stunts from helicopters or cable cars, and, of course, the humour. It is a style that has audiences biting their nails one minute and laughing aloud the next as the action moves apace from scene to scene. This, then, is James Bond 007 in the cinema, a 25-year-old institution with – we hope – no end in sight.

A proud producer – Albert R. Broccoli – relaxes on the construction site for the world's largest stage, built on his initiative at Pinewood Studios for the filming of The Spy Who Loved Me.

property, has mastered the microchips and miniaturization of the Eighties. And despite frequent changes of actor, Bond's CIA colleague Felix Leiter still turns up to assist from time to time.

The British, in the shape of M and, more recently, the Minister of Defence, have always been portrayed as a force for peace in the world, staving off the more warlike tendencies of their American or Soviet counterparts. In order to preserve this attitude to détente, the early villains were never members of SMERSH, the Soviet Secret Service which went in for murder in Fleming's books, but operatives of SPECTRE, a freelance organization whose initials stand for Special Executive for Counterintelligence, Terrorism, Revenge and Extortion. Its head, Ernst Stavro Blofeld, graced many of the earlier films. Later villains have worked more on their own, though often related to the KGB somewhere in the past, with their own private plans for world destruction. General Gogol of Soviet Intelligence, a comparatively recent addition to the standing cast, is another character who, like M, is determined to preserve détente at all costs. In *The Living Daylights*, Gogol receives promotion to the foreign service.

At the beginning Fleming's novels had a largely British following, but by 1960 they had gained an international readership. Their worldwide sales increased dramatically on the release of the film of *Dr No* in 1962 (which coincided with President Kennedy's statement that Fleming was on his light-reading list).

The films have attracted new fans and have tended towards a concept that Albert R. Broccoli and Harry Saltzman, the original producers of the series, once described as 'total cinema'. In terms of James Bond, this translates as family entertainment,

The James Bond Team

Ian Fleming

The creator of James Bond, Ian Fleming was born in 1908 to an upper-class family. He was educated at Eton and then spent two years at the Royal Military College, Sandhurst. He resigned his commission in 1927 and then went to the Universities of Munich and Geneva. Later, he carved out a career for himself in journalism, joining the Reuters News Agency where his facility for languages and interest in travel stood him in good stead. During the Second World War, he worked in Naval Intelligence which provided much of the background material for the Bond novels.

After the war, he returned to journalism and bought 6 hectares (15 acres) of land on the north coast of Jamaica where he retired each year to write the Bond novels at his house, Goldeneye. From 1953, he wrote twelve Bond novels and eight short stories, nearly all of which have now been made into films. He died of a heart attack in 1964, before the release of *Goldfinger*, never knowing how successful the film series was to become.

Albert R. Broccoli

Known to everybody as 'Cubby', Albert R. Broccoli was born in 1909 in Astoria, Long Island. He entered the family business when he was 16, driving trucks of vegetables to market. (His uncle was the man who introduced broccoli to America.) He worked at a funeral parlour (coffins were, for a time, a recurring in-joke in the Bond series) before obtaining a job as a mailboy at Twentieth Century-Fox. His rise through the ranks of the film business (he was an assistant director on Howard Hawkes' *The Outlaw*) was interrupted by the Second World War, during which he became an officer in the Coast Guard. After the war, he went into partnership with Irving Allen to form Warwick Films in

London which specialized in Anglo-American movies such as *Hell Below Zero*, *The Red Beret*, *The Trials of Oscar Wilde* and *Fire Down Below*. In 1961, he joined forces with Harry Saltzman to obtain the rights to the James Bond novels and he has been the major driving force behind the films ever since.

Harry Saltzman

The co-producer of the Bond series up to and including *The Man With the Golden Gun*, Saltzman was born in 1915 in Quebec. His family moved to the USA when he was quite young and he left his circus and vaudeville background for films after the war. He went into association with playwright John Osborne and director Tony Richardson to form Woodfall Films, the company responsible for many of the 'new wave' British films of the Sixties including *Look Back in Anger* and *Saturday Night and Sunday Morning*. Throughout his partnership with Broccoli, Saltzman continued working elsewhere, producing films such as *The Ipcress File* and *Battle of Britain*. His long-running partnership with Broccoli ended in December 1975 when he sold his interest in James Bond to United Artists.

Ian Fleming chats with Sean Connery and Shirley Eaton during a visit to Pinewood Studios while *Goldfinger* was being shot. Fleming died shortly before the film's release, never knowing how popular the films based on his novels were eventually to become.

Above *Producers Albert R. Broccoli and Harry Saltzman take a break with their new star of the Bond series, Roger Moore, during location filming for* Live and Let Die.

Below *Producer Michael G. Wilson in climbing safety gear takes a break with the newest Bond, Timothy Dalton, on location in Gibraltar for* The Living Daylights.

Michael G. Wilson

The current co-producer of the Bond series, Michael G. Wilson, studied electrical engineering and then law at college. He became a partner in a prestigious American law firm and began his association with Eon Productions in a legal capacity in 1972. His many talents have contributed to the Bond films in different ways – he co-wrote four of the latest Bond movies, including *The Living Daylights*, was the assistant to the producer on *The Spy Who Loved Me*, the executive producer on the next three films of the series and eventually became the co-producer on *A View to a Kill*.

'My name is Bond . . .

Sean Connery

Before James Bond, Sean Connery was a little-known actor at the start of his career. He had had some starring roles but suffered from continual miscasting. By the time he finally left the Eon Bond series, after *Diamonds Are Forever*, he was both a household name and an actor of international repute. Born in Edinburgh in 1929, the son of a truck driver, Connery worked at a variety of oddjobs – from bricklayer to milkman – before he landed a part in the chorus of the British stage production of *South Pacific* which began his career in show business.

With his leisurely smile, dead-pan wit and impassive manner, Connery epitomized the early Bond to such an extent that it seemed impossible to replace him. Worried about typecasting, however, he left the Eon series in 1971 and continued a highly successful career on the screen.

George Lazenby

Playing Bond in *On Her Majesty's Secret Service* allowed George Lazenby to move from a career in advertising to one in the movies. Born in Australia in 1939, Lazenby started his career as a model and moved into TV commercials for products such as Big Fry and BP. He remained in films, after his brief flirtation with Bond, in productions such as *The Man From Hong Kong* and *Saint Jack*.

. . . James Bond'

Roger Moore

Although Roger Moore's name was mentioned in the original Bond casting search, his commitment to the TV series *The Saint* prevented him being seriously considered for the role. But he did eventually take over from Connery in 1973 with *Live and Let Die* and brought his own touches to the role of 007. Although older than Connery – Moore was born in 1927 – he nevertheless brought a youthful charm to the part. He had established a reputation in TV series like *Maverick*, *Ivanhoe* and *The Persuaders* for combining action and light comedy. His Bond, which really came into its own with *The Spy Who Loved Me*, was more relaxed and lighter than Connery's and he brought a tongue-in-cheek humour to the series which gave the films a different dimension as they developed. He also continued to work outside the series, appearing in such action thrillers as *The Wild Geese* and *North Sea Hijack*. He was in seven Bond films in all, spanning a period of 12 years which ended with *A View to a Kill* released in 1985.

Timothy Dalton

Dalton first gained international recognition in the award-winning film, *The Lion in Winter*, in which he portrayed the young Philip the second of France.

His first love was the theatre and, after attending the Royal Academy of Dramatic Art (RADA), he spent a period in repertory. Following that, his commanding presence combined with his fine acting ability quickly established his reputation as a Shakespearian actor of note while starring with the Royal Shakespeare Company. Dalton's early film career included starring parts in *Wuthering Heights*; *Mary, Queen of Scots* and *Cromwell*. He also starred with Dustin Hoffman and Vanessa Redgrave in *Agatha*. More recently he starred in *The Doctor and the Devils* and *Brenda Starr*. His TV successes have included such diverse subjects as *Jane Eyre*, in which he played Rochester, *Sins*, and *Mistral's Daughter*.

His most recent stage acclaim was for his performances opposite Vanessa Redgrave in *Anthony and Cleopatra* and *The Taming of the Shrew* at the Haymarket Theatre, London.

Other Actors

Character actor Bernard Lee played M throughout the Bond series until his death shortly after the release of *Moonraker*. He was born in 1908 into a show-business family and went to the Royal Academy of Dramatic Art before establishing himself in films and theatre and later TV. He was replaced as M by Robert Brown, another distinguished character actor, in the more recent films, starting with *Octopussy*.

Canadian actress Lois Maxwell, who was the longest-running member of the Bond cast, played Miss Moneypenny in all the Eon Bond films until *The Living Daylights*. She began her acting career as a teenager, keeping her performances secret from her parents. She lied about her age in order to entertain the troops during the war and went to RADA afterwards. She entered films with *That Hagen Girl*, starring Shirley Temple and Ronald Reagan (she won the Golden Globe award for Best Newcomer) but her best-known part will always be in the Bond series. Caroline Bliss replaces Lois Maxwell as Miss Moneypenny in *The Living Daylights*.

Desmond Llewelyn has appeared in every Bond movie except *Dr No* and *Live and Let Die*. Born in Wales, he made his movie debut in a Will Hay film in 1939 and continued a steady career ever since. As Q, the eccentric inventor of the British Secret Service's gadgets, he has created perhaps his most memorable role.

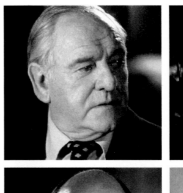

Bernard Lee (top left) *played M until his death in 1979; he was replaced by Robert Brown* (top right). *Walter Gotell* (above left) *plays the Russian General Gogol, who has been promoted to the foreign service in* The Living Daylights. *Geoffrey Keen* (above right) *appears in all the later Bond films as the Minister of Defence.*

In addition, Walter Gotell, an actor of international repute, now regularly appears as the Russian General Gogol (promoted to the foreign service in *The Living Daylights*). Now in his sixth Bond film, Geoffrey Keen plays the British Minister of Defence. Keen, another graduate of RADA, is a well-known figure in British cinema with a career that has spanned nearly fifty years from Carol Reed's *Odd Man Out* to *The Living Daylights*.

The Scriptwriters

Like Broccoli, Richard Maibaum, who has written most of the Bond scripts, was born in New York in 1909. He studied law and began writing for radio. He worked as an actor for a time in New York's Shakespearian Repertory Company. After his first Broadway play, *Sweet Mysteries of Life*, he was sought after by Hollywood and wrote several scripts for MGM and Paramount (including *They Gave Me a Gun* and *The Great Gatsby*). His screenplay for *Hell Below Zero* brought him into contact with Broccoli and he has since scripted many of the Bond films. His talents have been combined with those of co-producer Michael G. Wilson at the core of the most recent films.

Others who have contributed their talents to Bond film scripts include Roald Dahl, Christopher Wood, Tom Mankiewicz, George MacDonald Fraser, Paul Dehn, Berkley Mather and Johanna Harwood.

Above left *The ever-faithful Miss Moneypenny (Lois Maxwell) nurses a secret hope that one day she will be 007's date. Lois Maxwell's departure from the series after* A View to a Kill *leaves producer Albert R. Broccoli as the only member of the team to be involved in all of Eon's James Bond productions.*

Above right *Just occasionally Q (Desmond Llewelyn) leaves his office to get entangled in the action. In* Octopussy *he flies to the rescue in a hot-air balloon to help Octopussy's all-girl army get its revenge on Kamal Khan.*

The Directors

Terence Young, a screenwriter turned director, was responsible for three of the early Bond films including the very first one, *Dr No*. His taut, thriller style was inappropriate for the later movies and he continued to direct action movies such as *Wait Until Dark* and *Red Sun* elsewhere.

Guy Hamilton, who started in films as Carol Reed's assistant, has four Bond films to his credit. He has since directed several all-star productions including *The Mirror Crack'd* and *Evil Under the Sun*.

Lewis Gilbert, a veteran of British war movies such as *Reach for the Sky* and *Carve Her Name With Pride*, took on three Bonds. He entered the comedy arena with his recent film, *Educating Rita*.

Peter Hunt graduated from being the editor and second-unit director of the series to direct *On Her Majesty's Secret Service*. It was his only Bond film as director and he continued his career with such TV movies as *The Beasts Are on the Streets* and *The Last Days of Pompeii*.

John Glen, the first director to be responsible for four Bond films in a row, also came up through the ranks. A renowned editor of TV action series – *Danger Man*, for example – he became the editor and second-unit director on the Bond films and was responsible for the ski chases in *On Her Majesty's Secret Service*, the famous ski jump in *The Spy Who Loved Me* and the parachute stunt in *Moonraker*. He also directed action sequences in films like *The Wild Geese* and *The Sea Wolves*. Glen has stamped his own mark on the later Bond movies, evolving a flowing style which combines action sequences and story development without losing the film's pace.

Below left *Director Terence Young rehearses Ursula Andress on location in Jamaica for* Dr No.

Below centre *Guy Hamilton, the director of* The Man With the Golden Gun, *advises Britt Ekland on her role as Mary Goodnight.*

Below right *Lewis Gilbert, seen here on location for* The Spy Who Loved Me, *also directed* You Only Live Twice *and* Moonraker.

Director Peter Hunt takes a break with actress Ilse Steppat during the filming in Switzerland of On Her Majesty's Secret Service.

Perched above Paris on the Eiffel Tower, director John Glen (centre) discusses a shot with second-unit director Arthur Wooster (left) for A View to a Kill.

13

The Production Designers

German-born Ken Adam was the designer responsible for creating the look of the Bond films which helped make the series so successful. His futuristic sets have graced a range of other films including *Dr Strangelove* and his period designs for *Barry Lyndon* won him an Academy Award. Syd Cain alternated with Adam in designing some of the earlier Bond movies, including *From Russia With Love* and *On Her Majesty's Secret Service*, and was noted for his harsh, realistic sets.

Recently Peter Lamont has brought his own 'look' to the Bond series. He is another member of the Bond team who climbed up through the ranks, starting as a draughtsman on *Goldfinger* and working as an assistant art director, set decorator and art director before becoming the production designer on *For Your Eyes Only*. He has also won much acclaim for his designs for the recent science-fiction thriller *Aliens*.

Right *Ken Adam, one of the Bond series' production designers, on a part of his high-tech space-station set for* Moonraker.

Below *Production designer Peter Lamont in front of* Octopussy*'s bed, one of his gloriously flamboyant creations for that film.*

Effects and Stunts

Other regular members of the Bond crew include: John Stears, who won Academy Awards for his special effects work on *Thunderball* and *Star Wars*; Derek Meddings (the man credited with making *Superman* fly) who created many of the models and visual effects for the films; John Richardson, who has worked in special effects on projects as complex as *A Bridge Too Far*, *Superman* and *Aliens*; John Jordan, whose aerial photography has graced many of the Bond films; Willy Bogner, with his unrivalled ski photography, and Bob Simmons, a regular member of the stunt team, who has done everything from doubling for Bond to organizing entire stunt sequences.

Titles and Music

Maurice Binder has designed most of the main titles of the Bond movies, including the famous Bond gunbarrel logo used to introduce every film. He was offered the job on *Dr No* after his titles for Stanley Donen's *The Grass Is Greener* which featured several cuddly babies on a lawn representing the actors and technicians of the credits. Binder's hallmarks – beautiful girls and a touch of eroticism – have adorned the titles of nearly all the subsequent Bond films.

John Barry, composer of many of the Bond soundtracks, comes from Yorkshire. His father owned a chain of cinemas there and Barry entered show business with his own band – the John Barry 7. He has been involved with the Bond series since the beginning and is a four-time Oscar winner (two for *Born Free*, one for *The Lion in Winter* and one for *Out of Africa*). He is now one of the best-known composers working in films.

Throughout the Bond series, popular singers and lyricists have been brought in for the title song. These include Shirley Bassey, Tom Jones, Lulu, Louis Armstrong, Carly Simon, Paul McCartney, Sheena Easton and Duran Duran.

Of course, each Bond film employs the talents of many more people – from actors to caterers, from drivers to builders, from publicists to hairdressers – than can be singled out. Those mentioned here are just a few of the most prominent who have left their distinctive mark on the James Bond 007 series.

Above *Composer John Barry has written the score for many a Bond film. He is also responsible for the original arrangement of the 'James Bond theme'.*

Right *Maurice Binder exhibits a section of the famous James Bond gunbarrel logo which he designed.*

DR NO

*The first James Bond film appealed to the critics and the public alike, establishing
Sean Connery as 007 and ensuring the continuation of the series.*

The first of the James Bond movies, *Dr No*, set the series off to a fine start. It is a fast, action-packed adventure located more in the real world than many of the later films. Director Terence Young was an avid reader of Ian Fleming; hence the *Dr No* film is more closely related to the novel than are many of the others. In particular, more of the workings of the British Secret Service – from the telephone room to brief mentions of standard issue equipment and Universal Exports as the cover operation – are in evidence. In London Bond's apartment is shown (it only appears in one other film to date – *Live and Let Die*), and in Jamaica, Government House is introduced – a rare reference to the links between the secret and diplomatic services. The result is to keep *Dr No* closer to everyday reality. As a film, it is both more violent and more cold-blooded than its successors, presenting 007 as a suave killer (albeit one who is irresistible to women) rather than the likeable agent of later Bond movies.

It is clear from the start that producers Harry Saltzman and Albert R. Broccoli intended *Dr No* to be the first of a series. Many of the key elements are already in place – like Bond's continual flirtation with M's secretary Miss Moneypenny, coupled with M's repetitive instructions to 'omit the niceties'. Several other ideas which began in *Dr No* were dropped in later films – for example, the Sylvia Trench character (played by Eunice Gayson) was originally intended to reappear in every film. It is Sylvia whom Bond is chatting-up in a casino when he is first introduced to the audience with the classic line – as he lights a cigarette – 'My name is Bond . . . James Bond'. She follows him to his apartment only to find that he has to hurry away on a mission. The idea was that in each Bond film Sylvia would be constantly disappointed as 007 had to rush off before he could make love to her – but the idea was dropped after *From Russia With Love*.

Felix Leiter, here played by Jack Lord of *Hawaii Five-O* fame, is another character introduced in *Dr No* who is included in a number of the subsequent films, played by a variety of actors. But this jovial, almost boyish CIA man from Texas, who appears throughout Fleming's novels to aid and abet Bond, has never been consistent in the films, although he appears again in the latest adventure, *The Living Daylights*, played by John Terry.

Other themes initiated for *Dr No* have proved

more successful. The film opens with a group of white dots travelling across the screen. They change into a view through a gunsight. A man steps into the sight, turns to face the audience and shoots. Then a red wash slowly drops down to cover the screen. This, by now world-famous, opening was designed by Maurice Binder – considered to be the best main title designer in the business.

Similarly, the distinctive 'James Bond theme' has remained with the series. Credited to Monty Norman who wrote the calypso-style music for *Dr No*, the theme was arranged by John Barry whose orchestra recorded the piece for *Dr No* for a mere £200 (less than $600 at the time). Both Binder and Barry have remained a regular part of the Bond team.

The Assignment

When agent Strangways disappears in Jamaica, M sends Bond out to investigate. Strangways had been checking out a US enquiry about interference that they have been experiencing with their rocket launchers from Cape Canaveral. Toppling, the art

Above *James Bond prepares to leave the casino where he has been playing with Sylvia Trench (Eunice Gayson) all evening. They agree to meet again to play a game of a different kind. But Ms Trench's expectations are never fulfilled because 007 has to hurry away on a mission.*

Left *Bond, as always, proves that he is a gentleman by protecting Honey (Ursula Andress) from Dr No's henchmen.*

Above *Bond has to cope with hazards as various as burning metal and torrents of water when he escapes from Dr No's prison cell through a ventilator shaft.*

Below *Quarrel (John Kitzmiller), Bond and Honey are here trying to throw Dr No's men off their track. Seconds later they are discovered and have to hide under the water.*

of throwing the gyroscopic controls off-beam by remote control, is suspected and it seems to be coming from the Jamaican area. With the moon launch approaching, the Americans need to be certain that nothing will go wrong, so 007 is sent into the fray.

Equipment Issued

Major Boothroyd (who in later films is known as Q) persuades Bond – with M's help – to change his gun. Bond is currently using a Beretta .25, scathingly described by Boothroyd as 'light enough for a ladies' handbag'. His replacement gun is a Walther PPK 7.65mm with an attachable silencer that produces little reduction in muzzle velocity when used. This gun was to become Bond's trademark throughout the series.

In general, there is very little gadgetry in *Dr No*, leaving Bond to rely more on his fists and his wits. For instance, he uses hairs across doors and powder on locks to check on unwelcome visitors rather than the sophisticated gimmicks that audiences would in

time come to expect. When he and his companions are cornered in a stream, he cuts reeds for them to breathe through underwater. The later Bond would have just happened to have some handy device – designed exactly to meet this situation – secreted in his back pocket. This lack of equipment is also the reason for the film's hard edge; in order to kill, Bond has to shoot in cold blood. The result of introducing the various gadgets was to temper the violence and make the series more entertaining for a family audience.

Enemy Personnel

Dr No

Operating from Crab Key off the coast of Jamaica, Dr No is the brains behind the misguided missiles operation. Coolly played by Joseph Wiseman, a New York stage actor of renown best known for his role in the stage and screen versions of *Detective Story*, Dr No is ruthless – his subordinates prefer to die than talk. The scriptwriters toyed with many ideas to bring Fleming's villain to the screen – including the bizarre notion of making Dr No a monkey – before giving him metal hands, his distinguishing mark in the movie.

Over a meal at Crab Key, Bond learns that Dr No was the unwanted child of a German missionary and a Chinese girl of good family. Despite his disadvantages in life, he rose to become treasurer of a Chinese Tong – it was a rare distinction for a non-Chinese to be allowed into the heart of one of these secret Chinese societies. But Chinese caution was justified when Dr No fled to America with $10 million of their money in gold. An engineer of note (he designed his headquarters himself) he is, of course, working for SPECTRE and the rocket interference is part of an unspecified plan for world domination.

There is a neat visual joke connected with Dr No's headquarters. When Bond first enters his dining room, he does a double-take when he sees Goya's picture of the Duke of Wellington which had been stolen a few months earlier. This was the first of many topical references that were to add sparks of humour to the Bond films.

Professor Dent

Unlike later villains, Professor Dent, one of Dr No's henchmen, is quite talkative and friendly – he was even a drinking partner of Strangways. He runs a laboratory in town and Bond picks up the scent when he finds some rocks of Strangways that Dent has incorrectly analyzed, hiding their radioactivity. Dent's express orders are to eliminate 007, which he first tries to do with a large tarantula. This scene was shot using the clever trick of placing a pane of glass between Connery's bare torso and the spider. His next attempt (007 easily disposed of the lethal arachnid) involves Miss Taro (a pretty secretary from Government House) who invites Bond to her cottage. As 007 can never resist an invitation from an attractive woman, he walks knowingly into a trap. So when Dent breaks in on the lovers, he wastes his shots by filling a bolster in the bed full of lead. Bond, on the other hand, puts his newly acquired Walther PPK with attachable silencer to good use.

The Bond Girl

Honey Ryder

The introduction of Honey Ryder has to be one of the best-known scenes from a Bond movie – indeed, from any movie. She emerges from the sea, clad in a skimpy white bikini with a hunting knife tucked in one side, singing 'Underneath the Mango Tree'. Her boat, which she regularly uses to get to Crab Key, has been holed so she has to stay with Bond for the remainder of the adventure, braving all sorts of real and imagined horrors at the hands of Dr No. Honey is a kind of natural innocent, in a sense the counterpoint to Bond's worldly sophistication. She is not a total stranger to violence, however, for in a previous episode of her life when her landlord had tried to rape her, she responded by putting a black widow spider underneath his mosquito net.

She is the daughter of a marine zoologist (killed by Dr No) and she lived with her father, travelling from place to place, receiving no formal education. From Bond, of course, she is destined to learn some of the facts of life.

Dr No (Joseph Wiseman) wishes James Bond were on his staff as he entertains his reluctant visitor to a lavish dinner.
Dr No's sneering superiority, his metal hands and his devious plan make him one of the most memorable of Bond's adversaries.

It was the famous picture of Ursula Andress in a man's wet T-shirt that led her to be cast in *Dr No*. In *Dr No*, her husky, accented voice adds to her characterization and her career was revived for a period. She went on to play similarly attired roles with Frank Sinatra and Dean Martin in *Four for Texas*, with Elvis Presley in *Fun in Acapulco*, with Peter O'Toole and Peter Sellers in *What's New Pussycat?* and in one of her best-known parts as *She* – the alluring immortal queen of novelist Rider Haggard's lost African City.

The Victim

Quarrel

Bond learns that Quarrel, a local fisherman, had been helping Strangways, taking him around the islands collecting rock samples. CIA man Felix Leiter helps Quarrel overcome his distrust of Bond and, despite his fear of the 'flame-throwing dragon' that he insists inhabits Crab Key, he takes them there. Bond dismisses his worries as island superstition only to discover that, at night, a flame-throwing tank looks remarkably like a dragon. Quarrel – as he himself feared – falls victim to the tank in one of the film's genuinely moving moments.

Quarrel is played by John Kitzmiller who lived and previously worked primarily in Italy.

The Background Story

Dr No's budget was $900,000 (then around £300,000) but United Artists agreed to $100,000 extra expenditure for the final spectacular set. The film repaid United Artists' backing from the British release alone which recouped a record-breaking £700,000. Despite its comparatively low budget, the film, which was shot at Pinewood Studios and on location in Jamaica, has the lavish feel of an expensive movie. Ken Adam's hand in the production design is clearly evident from the gleaming surfaces and weird angles (which are his trademarks) of many of the interiors. Take, for instance, the room where Dent is given his instructions by the disembodied voice of Dr No. It is a bare white room with a sloping ceiling and sinister shadows created by a criss-cross grill in the roof. On a table in the centre of this large, empty space is a small cage

Above left *Bond's sleep on the beach at Crab Key is disturbed by the appearance of Honey Ryder who is singing while she collects shells. The very first Bond girl here set the pattern for numerous amorous exploits in future films; but even 25 years later, this vision of Honey remains one of the most memorable Bond-girl images.*

Left *Quarrel finds his worst fears realized when he comes face to face with a 'fire-breathing dragon' on Crab Key.*

containing the tarantula. The whole creation adds to the menace of the scene.

But the most impressive set in the film – and also the only one which makes a marked departure from any kind of realism – is that created for Dr No's headquarters and underground atomic plant on Crab Key. In its rusty, muted browns the above-ground buildings have the feel of a decaying factory while below stairs all is glistening new high-tech. If the details of the operation of nuclear energy now seem outdated it is not because of any lack of understanding on the part of the film-makers. The decontamination scene, for instance, where Bond and Honey are washed free of radiation, now looks rather facile. At the time it was as good a scientific approximation as had been seen on the screen.

The laboratory, with its banks of scientific equipment – on loan from British research companies and worth an estimated £100,000 (around $275,000), at that time a lot of money – and central reactor pool which bubbles and boils as over-hanging rods are pushed in and out, has a threatening air to it. As Bond and Dr No slug it out among the equipment, special scientific technicians had to be on hand to protect the expensive machinery. Inevitably, Dr No suffers a fitting end, falling into the core and unable to pull himself out again because of his metal hands. By now, the core is about to blow (the term 'melt-down' had clearly not been coined by that time) and Bond and Honey have to escape before it goes up. Thus were born two more-or-less standard elements of Bond movies – the cataclysmic explosion of the villain's headquarters at the climax of the film and the subsequent escape of Bond and his chosen companion to relish their victory somewhere undisturbed.

Above *Dr No's underground laboratory, which harnesses atomic power as a means of interfering with the launch of American rockets, is in trouble. The reactor pool is suffering from an overload, and the first villain's headquarters of the series is about to blow.*

Below *In the final scene of* Dr No, *Bond gives a new twist to a classic ploy – running out of fuel. 'What are we going to do now?' innocently enquires Honey.*

DOSSIER

007 DR NO 1962 109 minutes

Producers
Harry Saltzman, Albert R. Broccoli
for Eon Productions

Director
Terence Young

Scriptwriters
Richard Maibaum, Johanna Harwood,
Berkely Mather

Director of photography
Ted Moore

Production designer
Ken Adam

Special effects
Frank George

Editor
Peter Hunt

Main title designer
Maurice Binder

Music
composed by Monty Norman,
orchestrated by Burt Rhodes,
conducted by Eric Rodgers.
'James Bond Theme' played by
John Barry & Orchestra

Distributor
United Artists

Cast includes
Sean Connery (James Bond)
Ursula Andress (Honey Ryder)
Joseph Wiseman (Dr No)
Jack Lord (Felix Leiter)
Bernard Lee (M)
Anthony Dawson (Professor Dent)
John Kitzmiller (Quarrel)
Zena Marshall (Miss Taro)
Eunice Gayson (Sylvia Trench)
Lois Maxwell (Miss Moneypenny)
Peter Burton (Major Boothroyd)

Locations
filmed on location in Jamaica
and at Pinewood Studios, England

FROM RUSSIA WITH LOVE

Even today, with its taut thriller style, this remains one of the most popular of the Bond films.

The second film of the Bond series, *From Russia With Love* is another fast-paced realistic spy thriller. In fact it is the last Bond film to take itself at all seriously. From *Goldfinger* onwards, there is always a tongue-in-cheek element that comes into play. Following on from *Dr No*, the film strengthens the Bond formula and adds a new facet to the presentation – the pre-title sequence. These preludes to the main action (which often have little to do with the main plot) have become not only a standard feature of the Bond movies but also a regular one elsewhere, particularly in action-based TV series.

Many would argue that the pre-title sequence in *From Russia With Love* is the best one. It is dark, in a maze, in a garden and Bond is stalking or being stalked by a shadowy figure. After an initial skirmish, Bond's opponent catches him in a grip, draws a cord from his watch and proceeds to garotte our hero. As Bond falls down dead, massive lights go up and a man walks forward from the audience watching the scene. He bends down and removes a mask from the body, making it clear that it is not 007 who has bitten the dust. It has all been a rehearsal . . .

This scene was, in fact, shot in the gardens outside the restaurant of Pinewood Studios. The privet hedges have been retained in the same style as they are seen in the film and today they are a major point of interest for visitors to the studio.

The next new element follows immediately – the titles. Designed by Robert Brownjohn, the credits are projected onto the undulating body of a female dancer. It is a striking prelude to the main action which captures the dangerous and exciting feel of the Bond movies.

In addition, *From Russia With Love* is funnier than its predecessor. It has not yet quite developed into the distinctive Bond humour that audiences have grown to know and love but it is a significant move away from Fleming. The humour largely consists of Bond throwing in witty one-liners usually delivered fairly dead-pan by Connery immediately after some vicious act of violence. The effect is to defuse the situation, mitigate the cruelty and get the pace going again.

Some of the most memorable lines used in this way are: as Kerim Bey shoots a Russian emerging from a door concealed in a film poster featuring Anita Ekberg's face, 'She should have kept her mouth shut'; on a view of Tatiana's legs as seen through a periscope, 'From this angle, things are shaping up nicely'; on the crash of a helicopter which explodes into flames, 'I'd say one of their aircraft is missing'; and on Rosa Klebb's demise, the deadly poison on her toe-caps unused, 'She's had her kicks'.

The Assignment

Tatiana Romanova, a Russian cypher clerk, has said she will defect with a valuable cypher machine, known as a Lektor, if James Bond (with whom she has fallen in love) goes to Istanbul to pick her up. Unknown to M and 007, SPECTRE are behind this scheme. They have three motives: to set the Russians and English at odds with one another; to profit from the deal when they sell the Lektor back to the Russians; and to lure Bond to his death in revenge for killing their operative, Dr No. Even if the plot is somewhat transparent, it will work, they reason, because the British can never resist a trap.

Equipment Issued

Boothroyd, who is now designated head of the Secret Service's Q branch, has a new standard-issue device for all double-0 agents. It looks like an ordinary black leather case but it has 20 rounds of ammunition and 50 gold sovereigns concealed in different parts of its spine, a throwing knife released at the push of a button and a tear-gas bomb, disguised as a tin of talcum powder, designed to explode if the case is opened the wrong way. Inside the case is a folding sniper rifle, .25 calibre and equipped with a telescopic infra-red sight. Nearly all of this gadetry is used during Bond's lengthy fight with SPECTRE operative Grant on the train.

Enemy Personnel

Ernst Stavro Blofeld

From Russia With Love introduces Ernst Stavro Blofeld, the head of SPECTRE and always referred to as Number 1. Although his face is not seen in this

Left *Tatiana Romanova (Daniela Bianchi) may be new to the business of spying but she certainly knows how to lay a trap for James Bond. Above the bed is a two-way mirror through which her seduction of 007 is filmed for purposes of blackmail.*

film, he is immediately identifiable by the white cat that is always with him. We get to see more of him in later films.

Rosa Klebb

Blofeld's Number 3 is Rosa Klebb, a recent ex-head of operations for Soviet Intelligence (known as SMERSH). In a surprising bit of casting, German actress Lotte Lenya who was the widow of composer Kurt Weil plays Klebb. She made a name for herself in the Twenties as a singer – particularly in Berthold Brecht's *The Threepenny Opera* with music composed by her husband Weil.

Considered a beauty in her youth, Lenya gives a remarkable performance as the frumpily dressed, red-haired SPECTRE operative, her dedication to the overthrow of civilization evident in her every move. The poisoned spikes protruding from her shoes with which she tries to kill Bond in the final showdown are the ultimate material projection of her personality.

Above *A nice in-joke occurs when a hired assassin tries to leave his base through a trapdoor in a huge poster of Anita Ekberg's face. The poster advertised a film she had starred in titled* Call Me Bwana *which was co-produced by Harry Saltzman and Albert R. Broccoli.*

Below *Rosa Klebb (Lotte Lenya) visits SPECTRE's notorious training school where agents become skilled in target practice, karate, flame-throwing, judo and other murderous activities.*

Kronsteen

Number 5 in the SPECTRE hierarchy is Kronsteen, a chess grand-master responsible for master-minding the Lektor plan. (The chess tournament scene in *From Russia With Love* was ahead of its time in having boards for spectators to follow the game;

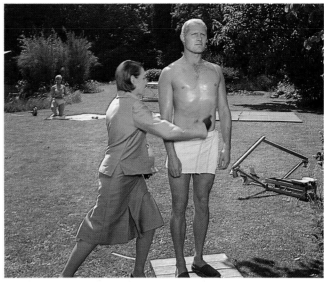

and although shot in the Sixties, it has a very Eighties feel to it). A thin-faced subordinate, played by Vladek Sheybal – one of the most prolific portrayers of villains in English cinema – Kronsteen is better at chess moves than spying. To be kicked in the shin with a poisoned toe-cap when the trap fails is his just reward.

Above left *As Kronsteen (Vladek Sheybal) takes black's bishop in the Venice International Grandmasters' Championship, he receives a secret message to contact headquarters immediately. So he has to win the game – fast.*

Above *Rosa Klebb, armed with her knuckleduster, finds Red Grant (Robert Shaw) in the peak of physical condition. His response to SPECTRE's training has been so satisfactory that he is chosen for the starring role in the plot to assassinate Bond.*

Below *Tatiana Romanova may think she is helping her country by obeying the dictates of Rosa Klebb. In fact, she is unwittingly aiding SPECTRE – a very different kettle of fish.*

Red Grant

The real villain of the piece is Red Grant, the assassin of the pre-title sequence. He is a convicted murderer who escaped from a British top-security jail in 1960 and was recruited by SPECTRE two years later in Tangier. As Klebb is told, his response to SPECTRE's training and indoctrination is remarkable and he goes on to display his fitness by not batting an eyelid when Klebb lands him a vicious punch in the stomach with her knuckleduster.

Grant's presence in the film is, at first, quite shadowy. However, the pre-title sequence is always an incisive reminder that he is dangerous. Throughout the story's opening stages he silently watches over Bond, protecting him – until the Lektor is safely out of Eastern Europe – by dispatching potential killers be they SMERSH agents or gypsies. He comes into his own – speaking his first words in a surprisingly upper-class English accent – on the train when he introduces himself to Bond in the guise of the Belgrade agent, Captain Nash.

Robert Shaw, the versatile English actor of stage and screen who played Grant, had to undergo training to acquire the physique necessary for the part. He and Sean Connery both had to learn the finer points of Turko-Grecian wrestling in a gymnasium in Istanbul for the fight sequences. It may be a far cry from Shakespearian acting, for which Shaw had a reputation, but his portrayal of Grant is one of the best villains of the Bond series.

The Bond Girl

Tatiana Romanova

The cypher clerk Tatiana Romanova is ordered to report to Klebb who is posing as a SMERSH agent. Klebb instructs her to help the KGB by undertaking an assignment to feed false information to the English. Tatiana shyly explains that she is not used to this kind of work, she trained for the ballet but had to give it up when she grew to 2.5 cm (1 in) more than regulation height. When Klebb insists that she cooperate, Tatiana accepts her orders which are – to put it succinctly – to fall in love with Bond.

The producers had searched hard for an actress who could believably play Tatiana. Daniela Bianchi had been in three Italian films, done a little TV and been the runner-up in the 1960 Miss Universe contest when she was spotted by the Bond casting scouts. She brings a convincing blend of innocence and guile to the part, smoothly effecting the transition from an agent doing her duty (seducing Bond wearing nothing but a black choker) to a woman in love (revelling in her new nightgowns). Of course, she gets the opportunity to prove her love is real by disobeying her orders (even if they were issued under false pretences) and saving 007 from the evilly kicking Klebb. Ms Bianchi married the president of a shipping company and retired from films shortly after the release of *From Russia With Love*.

The Victim

Kerim Bey

As Kerim Bey, Pedro Armendariz all but steals the show. Bey is Bond's contact in Istanbul who guides him round a city where everybody follows everybody with everybody's blessing. He is a likeable fellow, who began life breaking chains and bending bars in a circus and ended up as a British agent employing all his sons in key positions. He is frank in his questions and gregarious in his encounters – he even settles down to tell his life story to a SMERSH agent he has gagged on the train. Unfortunately, Grant once again silently intervenes and shoots both prisoner and warden.

Kerim Bey (Pedro Armendariz) being distracted from his work by his mistress (Nadja Regin) which is just as well, as his desk is blown up by his enemies a few minutes later.

In the girl-fight at the gypsy camp, Zora is played by former Miss Jamaica, Martine Beswick, and Vida by former Miss Israel, Aliza Gur. The fight involves hair-pulling, slapping, finger-bending and biting as the girls have no holds barred to win the man they both want.

One of the major set-pieces of *From Russia With Love* occurs when Kerim Bey takes Bond to a gypsy camp for safety. They arrive just before a girl-fight is about to take place. Two gypsy girls, Zora and Vida, competing for the love of the same man, attack each other with no holds barred in a remarkably vicious fight for a Bond movie. After a sudden attack on the camp (Grant saves Bond during the battle) Bond, who has rescued the gypsy leader from certain death, is asked what he wants for his reward. Despite strict instructions from Bey not to interfere, Bond asks for the girl-fight to be stopped. It seems that even 007 cannot stomach the violence of the spectacle. As a result, he solves the whole situation by being given the chance to choose which girl should get her man – after he has sampled, in typical Bond fashion, the delights of both.

Armendariz, a Mexican who was raised in Texas, had three successful careers in films – the first in Mexico, the second in America and the last in Europe. From a romantic lead to a character actor, he had tried his hand at it all. During the filming of *From Russia With Love*, it was discovered that he had cancer but he carried on filming despite being in great pain. The film crew was in awe of his courage on the set as he continued to act the part of the sociable Bey before collapsing after each take. He shot himself some months after the completion of the film in order to avoid a painful, lengthy death.

The Showdown

It is the acting, which is of the highest quality, that carries *From Russia With Love* through. It has none of the elaborate, futuristic sets of most Bond films and production designer Syd Cain, whose forte is working with real locations, was brought in. But it is the characterizations together with some pacy editing that keep the dynamics going. This is seen at its best in the lengthy journey on the Orient Express which covers over 20 minutes of screen time.

Bond and Tatiana are trying to cross the border with the Lektor but Grant and a SMERSH security man are – for different reasons – out to stop them. Grant, impersonating the Belgrade agent Nash, almost gives himself away by ordering red wine with fish but 007 does not catch on until too late. The resulting, carefully constructed fight – filmed with three cameras – has Bond using the gold coins to tempt Grant to open the case, the tear-gas bomb to distract him and the knife to release a stranglehold. When the lights are shot out halfway through, the fight is bathed in blue light – making it one of the most exciting in the Bond stable – as Bond defeats Grant and gathers up Tatiana and the Lektor to leave the train when it stops for a pre-arranged accident.

After neutralizing an enemy helicopter they head to where a speedboat is waiting to get them to Venice. But SPECTRE are still on their tail and four or five boats converge to block their escape. The special-effects department now comes into play as Bond pushes the speedboat's fuel cans into the lake, their contents spilling out through gun-shot holes. As he sets fire to the cans, boats crash into each other, people jump off burning craft and explosions rip the air. (Speedboat chases recur frequently throughout the rest of the series.)

There is no climactic explosion of the villain's headquarters in *From Russia With Love* but its finale

Pursued by a number of SPECTRE speedboats, Bond and Tatiana race across the bay headed for the Italian port of Venice in the last leg of their escape while stealing the valuable Lektor.

does bring all the ends of the plot neatly together. Bond and Tatiana are in their hotel, waiting to go home, when a maid enters. Tatiana quickly recognizes her as her assumed boss, Klebb, and stands watching helplessly while Klebb aims at Bond's ankles with her poisoned spiked shoes. But Tatiana comes through in the end, shooting her former boss before her kick can find its target.

The film remains tense and fast-moving throughout and it is perhaps its execution as much as its closeness to the original novel that makes *From Russia With Love* the Fleming fans' favourite Bond movie.

DOSSIER

007 FROM RUSSIA WITH LOVE 1963 116 minutes

Producers
Harry Saltzman, Albert R. Broccoli
for Eon Productions

Director
Terence Young

Scriptwriters
Richard Maibaum,
adapted by Johanna Harwood

Director of photography
Ted Moore

Production designer
Syd Cain

Special effects
John Stears

Stunt work arranger
Peter Perkins

Editor
Peter Hunt

Main title designer
Robert Brownjohn

Music
composed and conducted
by John Barry

Title song
written by Lionel Bart,
sung by Matt Munro

Distributor
United Artists

Cast includes
Sean Connery (James Bond)
Daniela Bianchi (Tatiana Romanova)
Pedro Armendariz (Kerim Bey)
Lotte Lenya (Rosa Klebb)
Robert Shaw (Red Grant)
Bernard Lee (M)
Eunice Gayson (Sylvia Trench)
Walter Gotell (Morzeny)
Nadja Regin (Bey's Mistress)
Lois Maxwell (Miss Moneypenny)
Aliza Gur (Vida)
Martine Beswick (Zora)
Vladek Sheybal (Kronsteen)
Desmond Llewelyn (Major Boothroyd)

Locations
filmed on location in Istanbul
and at Pinewood Studios, England

GOLDFINGER

The third Bond film, with its supervillain, high-tech gadgetry, glamorous girls and climactic ending, set the style for many future Bond movies.

This film, considered by many to be the highpoint of the early Bond films, lays down the blueprint for the remainder of the series. All the characteristic Bond elements are present and used to the full. There's the fast-moving, action-packed story which rarely pauses for breath, the evil villain bent on world destruction or domination with his seemingly invincible henchman, the unlikely gadgets with which Q supplies 007, the villain's lethal, high-tech weaponry (*Goldfinger* was one of the first films to use a realistic facsimile of a laser beam, the technique having been invented only three years earlier), the girls – good, bad and indifferent – and the inevitable car chase and explosive ending. Even a popular title song sung by a chart-topping performer (in this case a haunting Shirley Bassey ballad) became a recurrent feature of the Bond films.

In addition, *Goldfinger* introduces the characteristic Bond humour, in which film-makers and audience conspire together in laughing at the film. It is more pointed here than in either of the previous movies. The humour is most evident in the memorable pre-title sequence which opens with Bond swimming underwater with a seagull on his head for camouflage (a neat touch suggested by new Bond director, Guy Hamilton), proceeds via an explosion, a quick change from frogsuit to white dinner suit complete with red carnation – through to a girl and a fight. As Bond's opponent staggers backwards and falls into a bath, 007 – with appropriate quick-thinking – throws an electric fire in after him. As the would-be assassin frazzles in the water, Bond leaves the room muttering to himself (and the audience) 'Shocking . . . simply, shocking', and the complicity is immediately established.

The Assignment

The plot, too, is typical. Auric Goldfinger, the villain of the piece, is suspected of smuggling gold around the world and M sends 007 off, with bait in the form of a gold bar from a Nazi hoard, to find out how and why. Of course, that is not all there is to it and Bond learns that Goldfinger is up to something more sinister. Operation Grand Slam is his plan to explode an atomic bomb (made from cobalt and iodine) inside America's Fort Knox. This will not only contaminate the US gold supply for 58 years, thus increasing the value of Goldfinger's own considerable holdings, but also wreck the American economy into the bargain (which is why the Chinese are backing the plot).

Equipment Issued

To help him on his way, Bond is issued by Major Boothroyd (now and forever more known as Q) with the famous Aston Martin DB5 with its series of personal modifications. The car was, in fact, designed in conjunction with the Aston Martin manufacturers in Newport Pagnell, England, and many of the additions actually work. This perhaps accounts for its plausibility despite its almost endless list of gadgets – including rotating licence plates, machine guns behind the front lights, a passenger ejector seat activated by a red button in the gear stick, a tracking device in the glove compartment, a bullet-proof screen and the capacity to emit a smoke-screen or oil onto the road behind.

Bond proceeds to ignore the strict instructions from Q to return the car as he found it. In a well-conceived car chase early on in the film, Bond uses up most of the devices in trying to escape from Goldfinger's uniformed fleet of minions. This chase contains one of the best-loved scenes from a Bond movie when 007 utilizes the red button in the gear

Above *James Bond's famous Aston Martin DB5 was auctioned at Sotheby's in New York in 1986. It fetched $300,000 (around £210,000 at the time) – a fitting testament to its importance in the world of 007.*

Left *Bond finds golden girl Jill Masterson (Shirley Eaton) dead on his bed. Middle-Eastern belly dancers often paint themselves all over as part of their act but they always leave a small space unpainted to avoid dying of skin suffocation.*

stick of the Aston Martin and unceremoniously ejects his astounded passenger from the car. In spite of all the tricks, 007 is captured anyway and has to resort to Q's other offering – a small homing device which fits neatly into the heel of his shoe to let his colleagues know where he is.

Enemy Personnel

Auric Goldfinger

At first sight, Auric Goldfinger, with his thinning red hair and rotund figure, is an unprepossessing villain (however much he tallies with Fleming's original description). But veteran German actor Gert Frobe manages to establish quickly that he is an enemy of worth. Frobe had appeared in over 70 films when he took on the part but Goldfinger was his first English-speaking role. Following the Bond movie, he found a niche for himself in English-language film comedies such as *Those Magnificent Men in Their Flying Machines* and *Monte Carlo or Bust*. He also appeared in *Chitty Chitty Bang Bang*, based on a short story for children by Fleming, the only film produced by Broccoli alone outside the Bond series since its conception.

Goldfinger is obsessed to the point of madness with gold, admitting to Bond in an intimate moment that he has been in love with its colour and brilliance all his life. Indeed, that fact is evident from the time when his eyes light up at the sight of Bond's golden bar thrown at his feet during their introductory game of golf (filmed at the famous Stoke Poges golf course, only a few miles away from Pinewood Studios).

He has amassed his wealth through a crafty method of smuggling which conceals gold bars within the metal fabric of his Rolls-Royces. The cars are dismantled at his Swiss factory, revealing their hidden cargo.

Goldfinger's power is displayed to the full in the scene where he has elaborately planned 007's death by means of a laser beam which is slowly cutting its way between the legs of a spread-eagled Bond. Bond asks Goldfinger if he expects him to talk, to which the incorrigible villain replies, 'No, Mr Bond. I expect you to die'. He then nonchalantly turns away, not even bothering to stay and watch the outcome. Goldfinger earns his just rewards by being sucked out of the window of a plane during his final showdown with Bond.

Above *Goldfinger (Gert Frobe) threatens Bond with a laser beam. The laser gets its power from the amplification of light concentrated into a narrow beam so that it can sear through an 8 cm (3 in) block of steel in seconds. Later in the film a laser is used to cut through the door at Fort Knox.*

Right *At the climax of the film, inside Fort Knox, 007 has to contend with the precision hat-throwing of Oddjob (Harold Sakata) before he can attempt to disarm Goldfinger's atomic bomb. In a characteristic moment of quick-thinking, 007 realizes that while a steel-rimmed hat can decapitate it can also conduct electricity.*

Below *It seems that everyone is having a go at 007! Pussy Galore (Honor Blackman) is the kind of lady who is likely to treat Bond's advances as judo practice. But even she cannot predict the outcome of this particular romp in the hay.*

Oddjob

Goldfinger's henchman is equally formidable. Oddjob is a massive taciturn Korean who can parry any punch with his body. Even a gold bar that Bond throws at him in a desperate moment just bounces off. Oddjob has the impossible habit of killing people with his hat – a specially designed weapon made of steel which can even decapitate one of the stone statues that adorn the golf course. With fitting irony, it brings about is owner's timely demise when 007 manages to electrify the hat (stuck between metal bars inside Fort Knox) and Oddjob with it.

Actor Harold Sakata was, in fact, a Hawaiian wrestler billed as The Great Togo before he worked on *Goldfinger*. He had also won a silver medal for the USA in the light heavyweight weightlifting contest in the 1948 Olympics. As a wrestler, he was renowned not only for his knowledge of judo and karate but also for his coldly unexpressive countenance – a feature which obviously stood him in good stead for the equally unresponsive Oddjob. His role in this film changed his life, launching him on a successful career of TV villains in series like *Hawaii Five-O* and *Policewoman*. He died in 1982.

Honor Blackman, having been used to tough assignments as Cathy Gale in *The Avengers*, did many of her own stunts without a stand-in and this undoubtedly complements her very butch presence in the film. But with her TV image of a leggy, leather-clad action woman and her similarly active role in *Goldfinger*, Honor Blackman had a lot of difficulty throwing off the typecasting. It took her some years of moving between film and theatre to establish a different character and she now enjoys a reputation on the English stage in musicals like *Mother Goose*, *The Sound of Music* and London's West End production of *On Your Toes*. An unlikely end for a Bond girl!

The Victims

Jill and Tilly Masterson

The two Masterson sisters with whom Bond becomes involved while tracking down Goldfinger have less fortunate endings than Pussy Galore.

Bond meets Jill when she is helping Goldfinger to fix a card game by means of binoculars and a two-way radio. This equipment falls under Bond's control when she succumbs to his charms – and as a result Goldfinger loses the game. Bond later finds her on his bed covered from head to toe in gold paint, dead from skin suffocation.

Her sister is equally short-lived. She first meets 007 when she is trying to avenge Jill's death. Bond

The Bond Girl

Pussy Galore

The unforgettably named Pussy Galore is played by Honor Blackman fresh from the long-running TV series *The Avengers*. Ms Galore is first and foremost an ace pilot, indeed Goldfinger's personal one, who is training a squad of female aviatrix to spray a deadly nerve gas around the Fort Knox area to knock out the troops. She is also an iceberg who finds 007 eminently resistible and is more likely to land him a judo throw than a kiss.

Fortunately for both of them, Bond is never one to take rejection lightly; he keeps trying and his charm finally wins out. She changes sides at the eleventh hour, alerting the Pentagon to the impending danger to Fort Knox, thus providing Bond with some much needed back-up. But Goldfinger still has her in his power and when Bond is flown off in a private plane to receive his thanks from the President, Pussy turns out to be the pilot. Goldfinger enters the passenger lounge of the plane and, despite Bond's repeated warnings that it is dangerous to fire guns in planes, a bullet penetrates a window. In the ensuing chaos, caused by depressurization, Goldfinger is sucked out while Bond and Pussy abandon the plane to look forward to their awaited union underneath a parachute on the ground below.

Jill Masterson finds a novel way of playing Goldfinger's game – using binoculars and a miniature radio to spy on the opposition's card hand.

attempts to stop her becoming more involved by slashing her car tyres with a set of rotating blades which protrude from the hub-cap of the Aston Martin's wheels. But his efforts are to no avail and, even when they join forces, she soon falls victim to Oddjob's precision hat-throwing.

Shirley Eaton, who plays Jill, was an experienced child actress and hoped to use the movie to transform her image, casting off the girl-next-door tab for a sexier one. For Tania Mallet, who plays Tilly, *Goldfinger* was her first film and an opportunity to break away from modelling.

The Background Story

Goldfinger had a budget almost four times as big as that for *Dr No* and much of it is clearly evident in the lush and sometimes startling sets that adorn the film. Chief among these is the room at Goldfinger's Kentucky ranch where he reveals his plans to a bunch of hoods. At the start of the scene the room is a brown, barn-like space suitable for a country ranch. But almost everything in the room is mobile and by the time the walls have moved to reveal maps, the pool table has turned into an instrument panel and the floor has rolled back to uncover a model of Fort Knox, the whole area has been completely transformed into a modern operational headquarters.

Equally memorable is the set for Fort Knox, both the interiors and exteriors of which were built at Pinewood Studios. The outside is an exact full-scale model, complete with fencing and driveway, which, at the time, was one of the most expensive sets built at Pinewood. But it is the interior which is the *pièce*

Tipped off by Pussy, the US army are in a position to thwart Goldfinger when he tries to detonate an atomic bomb in Fort Knox.

de résistance. The production team was never able to penetrate the inside of Fort Knox on its reconnaissance visits there, so the whole set is a superb flight of fancy. Ignoring the fact that gold, because of its weight, cannot be piled higher than 75 cm (2 ft 6 in), gold is piled up to 12 m (40 ft) high in a spectacular concoction of gold bars and tubular chrome structures. With the metal polished until it shone when the lights were on it, designer Ken Adam created a glittering gold and chrome set which makes an ideal location for the film's big showdown with 007 battling against time to untangle himself from the atomic bomb (to which he is handcuffed), overcome Oddjob, foil Goldfinger's villainous scheme and set the world to rights once again.

DOSSIER

007 GOLDFINGER 1964 108 minutes

Producers
Harry Saltzman, Albert R. Broccoli
for Eon Productions

Director
Guy Hamilton

Scriptwriters
Richard Maibaum, Paul Dehn

Director of photography
Ted Moore

Production designer
Ken Adam

Special effects
John Stears

Action sequences
Bob Simmons

Sound effects
Norman Wanstall (Academy Award)

Editor
Peter Hunt

Main title designer
Robert Brownjohn

Music
composed and conducted
by John Barry

Title song
lyrics by Leslie Bricusse,
Anthony Newley,
sung by Shirley Bassey

Distributor
United Artists

Cast includes
Sean Connery (James Bond)
Honor Blackman (Pussy Galore)
Gert Frobe (Auric Goldfinger)
Shirley Eaton (Jill Masterson)
Tania Mallet (Tilly Masterson)
Harold Sakata (Oddjob)
Bernard Lee (M)
Cec Linder (Felix Leiter)
Lois Maxwell (Miss Moneypenny)
Desmond Llewelyn (Q)

Locations
filmed on location in Switzerland,
USA and at Pinewood Studios,
England

THUNDERBALL

This was the first Bond film to go beneath the waves and its stunning underwater photography ensured that these sequences would become a recurring feature of the series.

The story behind the screenplay of *Thunderball* is complicated, stretching over a number of years and a protracted legal battle. Before Saltzman and Broccoli were ever involved with James Bond, and before Fleming had written *Thunderball* (it was his ninth novel), discussions were already underway with various companies about making films or TV series from the Bond books. One interested producer was Kevin McClory of Xanadu Productions. He and Jack Whittingham collaborated with Fleming on a screenplay entitled *Longitude 78 West*.

When plans to turn it into a film fell through, Fleming went ahead and published the novel, *Thunderball*, based upon the story. He did not, however, acknowledge the story's source and McClory went to court to claim his due. The lengthy battle ended with a settlement in which McClory obtained the screen rights to the novel and he later joined forces with Saltzman and Broccoli (who had since bought the rights to most of the other Fleming books) to produce the film. Thus the fourth Bond film had a new producer.

Although Terence Young, who had directed *Dr No* and *From Russia With Love*, returned to the driving seat for *Thunderball*, the film has a very different feel to it. This is largely due to Sean Connery who, by now, has relaxed into the role, playing Bond with a studied casualness that makes him somehow more vulnerable and less remote than the hero of the earlier films. *Thunderball* was Terence Young's last Bond movie; he disliked the underwater sequences which he felt slowed the pace down, and he left the series saying that he would only come back to direct the very last Bond film. (McClory, incidently, turned out to be an underwater sportsman and his knowledge aided the filming of those scenes.)

Thunderball adds yet another new touch to the pre-title sequences, one that was to be used to great effect in the Roger Moore Bonds – the art of the miraculous escape. After the funeral of J.B., a SPECTRE operative, Bond meets the widow and punches 'her' in the face in an initially shocking move. Seconds later, all is revealed as Bond exposes the widow as a man – indeed, as J.B. himself – quipping in characteristic Bond fashion on his/her earlier exit from a car that, 'You should never have opened the door yourself'. (In Bond's world a woman would always wait for the door to be opened for her.) Then all hell breaks loose as SPECTRE

agents smash their way in and chase Bond on to a landing outside the building. He seems cornered but he has a perfectly tailored escape kit waiting in the form of a jet pack which propels him into the air, up and along towards his waiting Aston Martin DB5. The jet pack was, in fact, on loan to the filmmakers from the US army and as Bond remarks while on his flight, 'No well-dressed man should be without one'.

The Assignment

SPECTRE needs money. Despite its recent excursions into crime (which – in a topical reference to the hottest news story of the year – include acting as consultants for the British Great Train Robbery for a mere £250,000) SPECTRE is broke. But Number 2 has a plan – to hijack a Vulcan bomber while on a NATO exercise by substituting for the real pilot a SPECTRE agent who has undergone plastic surgery. The Vulcan has two atomic bombs on

Above *Bond polishes up the art of the perfect escape using his miniature jump jet to foil his attackers and descend from the château to his Aston Martin DB5.*

Left *Orange-costumed US aqua-paratroopers have been parachuted into the waters near Nassau in order to locate the stolen Vulcan aircraft and stop the evil Largo using its bombs. The traditional climactic battle of each Bond film is about to begin.*

Left *A rare look at SPECTRE's headquarters where all the top agents are making their financial reports to Number 1 (unseen). While Number 9 has got his figures in a mess, it becomes clear that it is Number 11 who has his finger in the till and he is despatched accordingly – frazzled in his chair and then dumped unceremoniously below the floor.*

Right *Fiona Volpe (Luciana Paluzzi), the 'kiss and kill' girl of* Thunderball *drives a BSA motorbike. Note in particular the rocket launchers fitted to the front fairing which make any bike ride with Fiona a deadly one.*

board which can then be used to hold Britain to ransom – for the sum of £100 million of uncut diamonds – against the threat of detonating the bomb in one of the major cities of the Western world. If the British accept the terms, then at six o'clock they are to arrange for Big Ben to strike seven times. The British are given two days in which to decide and all the double-0 agents are brought in for a conference on how to avert this disaster. Only Bond has a lead since, unluckily for SPECTRE, he was recuperating at the Shrublands health clinic when their agent was there undergoing plastic surgery. His lead takes him to Nassau in the Bahamas.

Equipment Issued

A rather tired and irritable Q arrives in Nassau to issue Bond with equipment when it becomes clear that the Vulcan bomber must be hidden somewhere underwater. He has a Geiger counter in a water-proof watch and an underwater camera that uses infra-red film to take pictures in rapid succession and which Bond uses to track down the bomber. For emergencies he has a (harmless) radioactive pill which acts as a homing device when swallowed (007 puts it to good use when he is stranded in an underground cave and needs to summon help – in the shape of Felix Leiter – to rescue him) and a pocket-size breathing device with a four-minute supply of air (just the thing when Bond is trapped in a shark-infested swimming pool!).

Below *Largo (Adolfo Celi) is the first Bond villain to have a team of henchmen specially trained for underwater activities. His inspection of the troops has more to do with diving suits and harpoons than guns and other military paraphernalia.*

Enemy Personnel

Emilio Largo

SPECTRE Number 2 is Emilio Largo, played with aristocratic presence by Italian actor Adolfo Celi. Celi's previous career included directing at the Brazilian Theatre in São Paolo, managing the Rio de Janeiro Opera Theatre and directing films and TV dramas before returning to acting. Thus he is one of Bond's more distinguished adversaries, and with his white hair and black eye-patch, Celi made the millionaire Largo distinctively debonair. Much later, Celi made his name with an equally villainous character – Pope Alexander VI, in the TV series *The Borgias*.

Largo operates from his luxury yacht, the *Disco Volante*, which not only houses a base for underwater operations in its hull, but also has the ability to shed its rear half and become a hydrofoil capable of speeds up to 150 km/h (95 mph). Production designer Ken Adam was proud of the construction of the *Disco Volante* which cost some £200,000 (then around $550,000) and involved souping up an old Mexican hydrofoil. Largo also has a mansion on the mainland where one of his pleasures is to keep a gang of Golden Grotto man-eating sharks (specially captured by Miami shark hunters for the film) to which he feeds the objects of his displeasure – including Bond.

Count Lippe

Largo's first assistant is Count Lippe. It is Lippe who gives the game away at the Shrublands Clinic when Bond is alarmed by the symbol on his arm – a red square with a line through it. He tries to kill 007 on a traction machine (affectionately known as 'the rack') but Bond gets his revenge by turning up the controls of the steam baths. As with all SPECTRE agents, failure is not tolerated and Lippe is dispatched.

Fiona Volpe

Largo's second assistant is the more deadly Fiona Volpe. She kills her first victim, Lippe, when he in turn is following Bond, with rockets fired from her motorcycle. She then turns her attention to 007. Fiona's seduction of Bond is memorable for the home truths she hurls at him, taunting him that he makes love to women in order to win them back to the path of honesty and virtue before discarding them. In that sense, she is determined to be one of

Bond's few failures – and she is. For Fiona is one of the only Bond women who is still trying to kill 007 (despite the intimate moments they have shared) when she meets her own death.

Bond has escaped from Fiona and her henchmen and the ensuing chase through the local carnival (the Jankanoo Parade – staged out of season in Nassau for the film-makers) leads them to the Kiss Kiss Club. Fiona dances with Bond as her accomplices try to get a clean shot at him. At the last moment, Bond pushes Fiona into the path of the bullet and she dies, recalling a similar move of his in the pre-title sequence of *Goldfinger* in which Bond, seeing an assailant reflected in a lady's eyes, changes the position of his embrace so that she 'gets it' instead of him.

Fiona is played by Italian actress, Luciana Paluzzi who started in movies with a walk-on part in *Three Coins in the Fountain*. *Thunderball* made a name for her as a sex kitten and she continued her career – being compared by the European press to Sophia Loren and Claudia Cardinale. *Thunderball* was one of her first English-speaking roles.

Right When the Disco Volante *falls apart, the front becomes a fast-moving hydrofoil while the heavily armed aft section fights a rearguard battle to foil Largo's pursuers.*

The Bond Girl

Domino

Claudine Auger, a former Miss France, is Domino, Largo's companion on the *Disco Volante* and the sister of the stand-in Vulcan bomber pilot. She had started in films in Jean Cocteau's *Le Testament d'Orphée*, then trained at the Théâtre Nationale before she was picked out for the Bond film which really launched her into European movies. Bond first meets Domino when she is diving for shells – recognizing the two moles on her left thigh from a photograph. He consolidates the relationship at a casino where he refrains from fleecing Largo (and thereby proving his expertise at the gaming tables) in order to dance with her. The affair continues in the water as well as on dry land and it is clearly love at first sight for Domino. When Bond discovers the body of her brother in the Vulcan bomber she naturally changes sides (incurring Largo's violent wrath) but finally helps to bring the SPECTRE

Above *As Largo steers the* Disco Volante *away from the action, Bond makes his move. But while the two battle it out, who is driving the boat?*

Below left *Domino (Claudine Auger) poses on the deck of the* Disco Volante. *When Bond first encounters her there is some confusion about her status – is she Largo's niece, his ward or his mistress? Whichever, she is also sister of the murdered Vulcan pilot, so Largo needs to keep a close eye on her.*

operative to justice by intervening at a crucial moment in the showdown between Bond and Largo aboard the *Disco Volante*.

The Victim

Paula

Unlike most Bond movies, the victim does not play a major role in *Thunderball*. Paula is the British agent on the spot who helps Bond to make contact with Domino. She falls prey to Fiona and swallows a tab of cyanide in order not to talk under torture. This brief part was played by Martine Beswick, the first of the Bond girls to appear in two Bond films. Beswick, a Jamaican-born model, was initially brought to the producers' attention for *Dr No*. She did not get a part in the film but did become Zora, one of the gypsy girls who appear briefly in *From Russia With Love*. And even her role in *Thunderball* is quite short!

The Background Story

As always, the production design on a Bond movie deserves comment. Besides the large amount of underwater filming, two of the *Thunderball* sets are memorable and contribute to the lore of the Bond stories. First there is the SPECTRE boardroom where details of the financial deals are revealed – while up on a dais Blofeld sits stroking his omnipresent white cat. All gleaming high-tech with black leather, tubular-structured chairs, the boardroom is

an archetypal villain's den. When the still unseen Number 1 wishes to dispose of a bungler, all he has to do is press a button and the sinner is electrocuted and his body disposed of. The cold metallic impact of the room adds to SPECTRE's menace. By contrast, the British Secret Service conference room is done out in green plush, marble pillars and tiled floors, reminiscent of the Empire in its splendour. It is also, of course, highly old-fashioned, emphasizing that – for the British – the old virtues are the best.

Many consider the highlight of *Thunderball* to be its underwater photography. Ivan Tors Underwater Studios Ltd were brought in to film these scenes which make good use of the expertise of cameraman Lamar Boren (who has developed his own equipment for underwater filming) and director Ricou Browning who has a whole complicated set of arm and hand signals to direct his team. Both men had previously worked on TV films like *Sea Hunt* and *Flipper* and have the best working underwater knowledge of the Bahamas – having filmed there for many years. A whole range of special equipment was designed for the underwater scenes including a two-man submarine, a sub-surface jet pack, sea sleds with rapid-fire compressed-air harpoons and a new method of submarine camouflage.

Early on in the film there is a remarkable scene when the Vulcan bomber lands in the sea. As it sinks to the seabed, dozens of SPECTRE operatives converge on the plane to cover it with specially designed camouflage netting. As an introduction to underwater scenes in the Bond movies, it is excellent.

With a 32-person camera team and 45 scuba divers as extras, the climactic underwater battle is spectacular. Orange and black frogmen fight it out with harpoons, knives (to cut the breathing apparatus) and carbon-dioxide guns, while various kinds of exotic fish – from stingrays to sharks – get mixed up in the action. Although *Thunderball*'s budget was almost seven times that for *Dr No*, it is easy to see where the money went. With John Barry's score underlining the tension, the underwater battle is a fitting climax here and went on to become another regular highlight of Bond films.

Right *Knives present a different threat when breathing apparatus is involved! The best action scenes in* Thunderball *take place underwater. To help identification and avoid confusion, Largo's men are wearing black frogsuits while the US aqua-paratroopers are dressed in orange.*

DOSSIER

007 THUNDERBALL 1965 129 minutes

Producer
Kevin McClory for Eon Productions

Executive producers
Harry Saltzman, Albert R. Broccoli

Director
Terence Young

Scriptwriters
Richard Maibaum, John Hopkins based on an original story by Kevin McClory, Jack Whittingham and Ian Fleming

Director of photography
Ted Moore

Underwater sequences
Ricou Browning, Lamar Boren

Production designer
Ken Adam

Special effects
John Stears (Academy Award)

Action sequences
Bob Simmons

Supervising editor
Peter Hunt

Main title designer
Maurice Binder

Music
composed and conducted by John Barry

Title song
lyrics by Don Black, sung by Tom Jones

Distributor
United Artists

Cast includes
Sean Connery (James Bond)
Claudine Auger (Domino)
Adolfo Celi (Largo)
Luciana Paluzzi (Fiona Volpe)
Rik Van Nutter (Felix Leiter)
Bernard Lee (M)
Martine Beswick (Paula)
Guy Doleman (Count Lippe)
Lois Maxwell (Miss Moneypenny)
Desmond Llewelyn (Q)

Locations
filmed on location in Paris, the Bahamas and at Pinewood Studios, England

YOU ONLY LIVE TWICE

In the fifth film of the series, Bond goes to Japan to confront –
for the first time – Ernst Stavro Blofeld in the flesh.

By *You Only Live Twice*, the Bond movies had been established as one of the most popular film series ever, with box-office takings going from strength to strength. But changes were clearly afoot. Connery was stating loudly and publicly that he was tired of playing James Bond. The producers offered him a large one-off payment to appear in this film – a successful move but only a temporary solution to the problem.

At the same time, a whole new range of talent was brought in, including a new director and a new scriptwriter. Lewis Gilbert, an experienced and versatile director with a wide range of films to his credit, was chosen. Peter Hunt, who had edited all the Bond films to date, became the second-unit director for *You Only Live Twice*, with responsibility for many of the action sequences, and went on to direct the next Bond film, *On Her Majesty's Secret Service*.

This is the first Bond film not to involve the writing skills of Richard Maibaum. Roald Dahl, a writer of children's books and bizarre short stories with his own unique brand of black humour, was asked to provide a script. The result is a Bond film with a difference: it is as hard-hitting as the early films but, at the same time, it is more fantastic in its storyline and its settings.

Dahl later wrote an article in *Playboy* magazine about his experience of writing a Bond picture. He was told, he said, that there are two cast-iron rules in Bond movies that cannot be broken. The first concerns the Bond character, which is fixed and unchangeable, and the second relates to the Bond girls and the order of their appearance in the film. The first girl should be pro-Bond and sacrificed early on in the plot (preferably in Bond's arms); the second should be anti-Bond but eventually succumb to his charms (if possible saving him from his enemies): the third must also be pro-Bond but circumstances should be such that the attraction is not consummated until after the adventure. Otherwise, Dahl recalled, anything goes! In fact, not all Bond films adhere to this formula, but Dahl did so with some interesting results.

The pre-title sequence is pure Dahl in its dark humour. After introducing the space motif which dominates the film, the scene changes to the Far East where 007 is trying out his charms on a Chinese girl. Suddenly the bed he is lying on springs into the wall, a gunman breaks in and plugs it full of lead.

There follows a naval funeral for Bond, after which the coffin is hauled up from the sea bed and opened on a submarine – and a very alive Bond seeks 'Permission to come aboard'. The vessel turns out to contain M, Miss Moneypenny and all the paraphernalia of the British Secret Service including the hatstand that 007 invariably uses for target practice. The whole incident has been a ruse to make Bond's enemies think he is dead.

The Assignment

Dahl introduced a space element into the plot that was not present in the Fleming novel – a timely decision given the news about the American manned space flight. US astronaut 'Buzz' Aldrin made his famous space walk from Gemini 12 while *You Only Live Twice* was in production.

SPECTRE are up to their tricks again. In midflight, an invader rocket intercepts an American space walk and literally swallows up the spaceship. The Americans believe that the Russians are trying to take control of space and so they threaten retaliatory action.

The British, however, think differently. Their sources suggest that the interceptor rocket came down somewhere in the Sea of Japan and they believe that a third party is involved. They are determined to keep the peace between the two super-powers.

As the next US launch is only three weeks away, 007 is sent off to Tokyo to investigate. He comes to suspect that Osato Chemical Engineering is a front for the astral kidnappers. Later, when a Soviet rocket is similarly gobbled up, the Americans still think that the Soviets are trying to pull the wool over their eyes and take a couple of steps nearer war. For the British peace-keeping mission, everything depends on 007.

Equipment Issued

Q is summoned to Japan to bring Little Nellie to help Bond in his search. On being unpacked from her four leather containers, she turns out to be a miniature one-man helicopter equipped with

Left *Blofeld, played by Donald Pleasence in* You Only Live Twice, *strokes his inseparable companion, his white Persian pussy cat.*

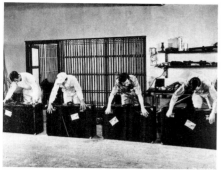

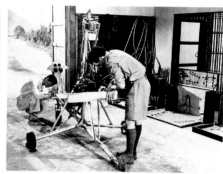

Little Nellie is assembled and made ready for battle by Q (Desmond Llewelyn) and his assistants.

She weighs 113 kg (250 lb), has a top speed of 208 km/h (130 mph), can fly at a height of over 4000 m (13,500 ft) and can travel for 2½ hours without refuelling.

No wonder SPECTRE's helicopters are no match for her with 007 at the controls!

typical Bond gadgetry. This comprises two machine guns with fixed ranges of 100 yd; two forward-firing rocket launchers; two flame-throwers; aerial land mines (to be used only when the target is directly underneath); and heat-seeking air-to-air missiles, firing at the rate of 60 per second.

This one-man autogiro was in fact the brainchild of RAF Wing Commander Kenneth H. Wallace. The producers saw it displayed on a TV programme, immediately obtained it for use in the film and kitted it out for Bond-style action. In *You Only Live Twice*, Commander Wallace performs most of the stunt work in Little Nellie himself. (Little Nellie can still be seen today, flown by Commander Wallace, at various air shows.)

Once she is unpacked, Little Nellie immediately goes to work. As Bond is making a reconnaissance flight over the Japanese islands, looking for SPEC-TRE's base, her shadow can be seen on the rocks below. Suddenly four more shadows appear and Little Nellie goes into combat with Bond displaying

his mastery of her multifarious devices to win a stunning victory.

This is one of the most exciting scenes in the film but Little Nellie (despite her expensive shipping from England) is used only once. While shooting that sequence aerial photographer John Jordan got his foot entangled with a helicopter blade. With amazing presence of mind (like a character in a James Bond movie), he trained the camera onto the damage in order to show the doctors what had happened. But it was to little avail and the foot was amputated when he returned to England. Jordan was back filming on the next Bond movie with an artificial leg. (A couple of years later, a particularly bizarre situation arose when a tight set for the film *Battle of Britain* only left a small space for the camera-man to get the shot. Jordan, of course, landed the job.)

Bond used only a few other gadgets in the film. There is a remarkable safe-cracking device which lights up as each coded number is found. Bond uses it to break into the safe at Osato Chemical Engineering.

Then there is the exploding cigarette – not one of Q's brainchildren, but a gift from the Japanese Secret Service. Blow down it and a miniature rocket missile shoots out. In a predictably tight corner, Bond requests the last cigarette for the condemned man – and the device comes into play.

Local Personnel

Tiger Tanaka

Once in Japan, Bond is assisted by Tiger Tanaka whose identity (according to Henderson – our man on the spot) is the most closely guarded secret in Japan. Tanaka is the head of the Japanese Secret Service and has all sorts of handy tricks to help him in his job. There is a chute which slides visitors (including Bond) into his presence; a private underground train (he remarks that he imagines M must have a similar arrangement); and a long-standing method of disposing of tailing cars (using a helicopter and a giant magnet to lift them off the road and into the sea).

He also has an army of trained ninjas, and when Bond has located SPECTRE's base, Tanaka takes him to his ninja training school to turn 007 into a Japanese agent. For this purpose Bond must know how to fight with staves, kicks, punches and karate. In order to be totally believable as a Japanese, Bond also has to acquire a hairpiece and a wife.

Right *Aki (Akiko Wakabayashi), in conjuction with Tiger Tanaka (Tetsuro Tamba), has a unique way of disposing of unwanted pursuers using a freight helicopter and a giant magnet. Those unwillingly picked up are then dropped into the sea.*

Below *Tiger Tanaka demonstrates the weaponry at his disposal to his assistant Aki and his esteemed visitor James Bond. However, Tanaka is not Q's opposite number but rather a kind of Japanese M.*

Tanaka is played by Japanese actor Tetsuro Tamba a veteran of over two hundred films and TV dramas. His best-known role in the West was as a guerrilla leader in *The Seventh Dawn* which was, incidentally, also directed by Lewis Gilbert. In *You Only Live Twice* he exudes a powerful presence which, even if he is a little young and smooth to be the head of a secret service bureau, makes him very convincing.

Enemy Personnel

Mr Osato

Osato Chemical Engineering turns out to be SPECTRE's cover in Tokyo. It is run by Mr Osato, a white-haired businessman who doubles up as a SPECTRE operative. His offices are expensive and elaborate, concealing such equipment as an X-ray machine disguised as a desk through which he can see that Bond is carrying a gun. He can also see, he says, that Bond smokes too much! Bond is currently posing as a businessman but Osato, aware of the gun, issues orders to have him killed. Unfortunately for Osato, he fails to recognize the gun as the renowned Walther PPK and thus underestimates how dangerous his visitor is. As always, the price of failure for SPECTRE agents is death.

Helga Brandt

Osato's secretary, Helga Brandt (otherwise known as SPECTRE Number 11), is girl number two of the Bond formula. She flirts with Bond, captures him and leaves him to die in a pilotless aircraft – he escapes. Her price for failure is to be unceremo-niously dumped by Blofeld into his tank of piranha fish.

Helga is played by Karin Dor who has been working in films since she was 16. She had a particular brand of 'good girl' image, especially on TV where she was forever playing the sweet, tough lady who always helps the hero to bust the gangsters. One brush with 007, and her image changed completely.

Ernst Stavro Blofeld

It is no surprise when the behind-the-scenes villain and planner of the escapade turns out to be none other than Ernst Stavro Blofeld, complete (as ever) with his white cat. But while in the first half of the film, Blofeld is his characteristic disembodied presence, towards the end of *You Only Live Twice* Bond – and the audience – finally gets to see him. British actor Donald Pleasence (substituted at the last moment when the Czech Jan Werich fell ill) plays Blofeld, another in the lengthy list of Pleasence's screen villains.

The make-up department spent a long time discussing how to make Pleasence look more evil, talking about humps, limps, beards and gammy legs. They finally settled on the scar which adorns Blofeld's face. Pleasence's voice has its usual sinister overtones and he acts with true menace, leading Helga to her death through a trapdoor in the bridge across the piranha tank, shooting Osato, trying to better Bond and, of course, interminably stroking the cat. He escapes on the monorail at his operations' base during the final battle and lives to fight another day.

Bond discovers that it takes more than a hairpiece to become Japanese when his sparring partner at Tiger Tanaka's training school turns out to be a SPECTRE assassin.

The Bond Girl

Kissy Suzuki

It is Kissy, an island diving girl who lives in the village where Blofeld's base is located, that Tanaka instructs Bond to marry. Mie Hama, who played Kissy, has been under contract to Toho Studios since she was 17 and had 67 films to her credit. *You Only Live Twice* was her first English-speaking part and she learnt the language for the film. She has never achieved such international prominence again in her film career.

Bond and Kissy go through a traditional Japanese wedding ceremony but, despite being married to the most eligible bachelor in the British Secret Service, she makes it clear that bedding Bond would be pleasure and not business – and therefore not done. She eventually gets her man – all according to the rules – in a floating raft at the end of the film.

Left *Kissy Suzuki (Mie Hama) and James Bond lie low to dodge a hovering helicopter which might betray their approach to Blofeld's headquarters in the volcanic Kirishima chain.*

Below *Bond and Kissy Suzuki are married in a formal multiple Shinto wedding ceremony as part of Bond's cover while he is masquerading as a Japanese fisherman in her remote village. Kissy is dressed in an ornate kimono with the traditional stiff white headdress.*

The Victim

Aki

Tanaka's assistant, Aki (played by Akiko Waka-bayashi), like every other girl in sight, falls in love with Bond. But she is not his usual kind of conquest being quite able to look after herself – and save 007 on more than one occasion. Driving around in her Toyota sports car (specially adapted for the Bond film by the Toyota Automobile Company) which contains a closed-circuit TV for contact with head-quarters, she is a very modern Japanese woman.

Unfortunately, she falls victim to SPECTRE in the end (remember – the first Bond girl always dies). Bond and Aki are sharing a bed the night before his marriage. A SPECTRE assassin climbs on to the roof and drops poison down a string poised over Bond's mouth. At the last minute, Bond turns over and Aki turns with him only to get the fatal dose straight into her mouth. It is an unusually moving moment.

Right *James Bond and Aki decide to spend their last night together knowing that Bond is getting married in the morning in the course of duty. It turns out to be Aki's last night alive.*

Below *Blofeld's operations' base is located inside a volcano in Southern Japan. This spectacular set, built at Pinewood Studios, had a rocket 20 m (66 ft) high which actually fired some 15 m (50 ft) above the gantry.*

The Background Story

The *tour de force* in *You Only Live Twice* is Blofeld's operations' base which is in the crater of a volcano fitted out with a massive green steel shutter which slides across the top to look like a lake.

At £400,000 (then over $1 million), this set at Pinewood Studios was one of the largest and most expensive ever built (giving Broccoli the germ of an idea for an extra-large 007 stage which he later built). It was a major achievement as it involved creating a whole crater complete with rocket-launching apparatus, a helicopter landing pad, a monorail for transporting people, and numerous elevators, cranes and so on. In fact, it was necessary to close this set when filming was in progress because so many of the technicians at Pinewood Studios came to marvel at it. It was one of Bond's most futuristic sets and when the 120-strong stunt team – divided between SPECTRE operatives in the red, yellow or white uniforms, and blue-grey ninjas, summoned by Kissy to help Bond – are ready to do battle it makes for one of the most exciting climaxes yet. The ninjas overpower the launch pad and penetrate Blofeld's control room, while Bond triggers the self-destruct mechanism on the interceptor spacecraft – seconds before it swallows another rocket. Peace, once again, reigns in the world.

Inside the volcano's crater, Tiger Tanaka's men, alerted by Kissy, penetrate Blofeld's operations' base and come to Bond's rescue.

DOSSIER

007 YOU ONLY LIVE TWICE   1967   110 minutes

Producers
Harry Saltzman, Albert R. Broccoli
for Eon Productions

Director
Lewis Gilbert

Scriptwriter
Roald Dahl

Director of photography
Freddie Young

Cameramen:
2nd Unit; aerial; underwater
Bob Huke; John Jordan; Lamar Boren

Production designer
Ken Adam

Special effects
John Stears

Action sequences
Bob Simmons

Second unit director
and supervising editor
Peter Hunt

Main title designer
Maurice Binder

Music
composed, conducted and arranged
by John Barry

Title song
lyrics by Leslie Bricusse,
sung by Nancy Sinatra

Distributor
United Artists

Cast includes
Sean Connery (James Bond)
Akiko Wakabayashi (Aki)
Tetsuro Tamba (Tiger Tanaka)
Mie Hama (Kissy Suzuki)
Teru Shimada (Osato)
Karin Dor (Helga Brandt)
Donald Pleasence
  (Ernst Stavro Blofeld)
Bernard Lee (M)
Lois Maxwell (Miss Moneypenny)
Desmond Llewelyn (Q)
Charles Gray (Henderson)

Locations
filmed on location in Japan
and at Pinewood Studios, England

ON HER MAJESTY'S SECRET SERVICE

*This Bond movie is doubly unique – it is the only one to star George Lazenby
and is the only one in which 007 marries for love.*

This is, of course, the first James Bond movie produced by Eon without Sean Connery in the starring role and it clearly showed that the Bond films could succeed (albeit differently) with someone else in the part. Directed by Peter Hunt, whose stated intention was to return the films to the spirit of the novels, this movie is a firm favourite among Fleming fans – even without the appearance of Connery.

The public at large, however, was less convinced. George Lazenby, an Australian model previously known for his appearance in BP commercials, is said to have won the part because of his credibility in the screen-test fight scenes. But he was not most people's idea of the suave, sophisticated and very British Bond, and although the film did good business at the box-office, its takings were not in the record-breaking league of the previous movies.

The pre-title sequence takes the bull firmly by the horns, gradually introducing the audience to the new Bond. As 007 is driving along in his Aston Martin DB5 (the last time this famous Bond car appears in the series), he stops to look at a girl on the beach who is heading directly into the water apparently bent on suicide. First of all his head is seen, then his silhouette, then quick flashes of his face. His entire face is not revealed until he has rescued the woman from the water and introduced himself with the (by now famous) line; 'My name is Bond . . . James Bond'. He then gets into a fight with two unidentified men and wins the skirmish, but as the girl drives away, rejecting his advances, he turns to camera, shrugs and says, 'This never happened to the other fellow!' It is a nice irony that sets the tone for what follows.

To emphasize the point, the opening titles recall images from previous Bond movies – people and places but never Connery. And to reinforce the change further, connections with the past are introduced in a later sequence. Bond, frustrated with M for removing him from the Blofeld case, dictates a resignation letter to Miss Moneypenny. While waiting for an answer, he goes to clean out his desk. It is the only time his office is shown in a Bond movie. (Incidentally, the number of Bond's office is 17 – a number that Broccoli has often been known to bet on.) In his desk are various memorabilia from the past – Honey's knife from *Dr No*, the watch with the garrot cord used by Grant in *From Russia With Love* and the miniature breathing device from *Thunderball*. And while Bond is examining his mementoes, John Barry's sound-track recaps some of the unforgettable themes from the series.

Bond is bewildered when M curtly grants his request, only to discover that Moneypenny took it upon herself to change the letter to ask for two weeks' leave. Both Bond and M (who was listening in) are duly grateful for her interference – after all, nobody really wants to lose 007.

There is one final humorous reminder of the previous Bond. At one point 007 passes a janitor who is jauntily whistling something vaguely familiar. It turns out to be the theme from *Goldfinger*. The era of the in-jokes in Bond movies had finally arrived.

The Assignment

On Her Majesty's Secret Service breaks all the carefully constructed rules of the Bond series – so much so that in this film there is no assignment. In fact, Bond is instructed by M to abandon his search for Blofeld, which is getting nowhere fast, and report for other duties. When he is given that two weeks' leave, however, he returns to Portugal to continue

Above *One of George Lazenby's strengths as the new Bond was his ability to stage realistic fights. This can be seen at its best in the pre-title sequence when he is attacked by a number of unknown hoods on the beach.*

Left *Tracy (Diana Rigg) becomes the first lady to win the hand of James Bond. For their wedding she is wearing a sleeveless, semi-diaphanous catsuit in organza and white guipure flowers covered by a voluminous three-tier coat of white organza with matching white boots.*

pursuing his obsession. He obtains a lead which suggests that Blofeld is trying to claim the title of Comte de Bleuchamp (Bleuchamp, as Bond points out, is Blofeld in French). He persuades a genealogist from the College of Arms to allow him to take his place and sets off to visit Blofeld disguised as Sir Hilary Bray.

This leads to some ripe tongue-in-cheek humour as Bond plays Bray at Blofeld's Institute of Physiological Research. In a clinic bulging with beautiful women who are there for allergy treatment, Bond has to act the part of a stuffy male uninterested in the other sex. The girls are a regular bevy of charmers (the first real gathering of beauties which was to become a hallmark of the Roger Moore films). They include Julie Ege, a former Miss Norway; Joanna Lumley, in transition from model to actress (she became the only actress to move from Bond to *The Avengers* rather than the other way round); Angela Scoular, fresh from Sixties' movies like *Here We Go Round the Mulberry Bush*; and

Sylvana Henriques, a former Miss Jamaica. His disguise does not deter Bond for long, however, and he is soon bedding at least two – and probably more, it is hinted – of the girls.

At the Institute he discovers that – as usual – Blofeld is up to something sinister. He has developed a virus which induces permanent sterility in particular breeds of animals and various strains of plants. He plans to spread the virus by means of the girls (armed with lethal atomizers) who are being unconsciously indoctrinated for Blofeld's ends. His intention is to hold the West to ransom, not for money (for once) but for a pardon for all his previous crimes and a recognition of his claim to the de Bleuchamp title. Once again, the future of Western civilization lies in 007's capable hands.

Equipment Issued

In another break with the Bond-movie rules, Q keeps a low profile in *On Her Majesty's Secret Service.* He appears at the beginning, chattering away about miniaturization and the discovery of radioactive lint which can be used as a tracer device. M wryly comments that at present the only person he needs to keep track of is 007 – and that is the last of Q for

> Disguised as Sir Hilary Bray, James Bond takes his daily constitutional with the girls of the Piz Gloria. Irma Bunt (Ilse Steppat) is to the right of 007 in dark hat and clothing.

When he played Bond, George Lazenby was renowned for doing all his own stunts. In this one he is escaping from the wheelhouse of the Piz Gloria where he has been imprisoned by Blofeld since his cover as Sir Hilary Bray was blown.

another film. The effect is, as before, to increase Bond's reliance on his fists which, in this film, are accompanied by loud echoing thuds whenever they are used. Lazenby insisted on doing many of the stunts and fight scenes himself, without a double. It is a decision that director Peter Hunt feels contributed greatly to the credibility of the fights.

Enemy Personnel

Ernst Stavro Blofeld

The object of Bond's quest, Ernst Stavro Blofeld, is played this time by Telly Savalas. With his round bald head and sharp New York accent, Savalas has taken on numerous powerful screen villains before Blofeld but, ironically, ended up best known for his lovable but tough TV cop, *Kojak*. In *On Her Majesty's Secret Service*, Blofeld's scar is there no longer; instead he has no earlobes – a defining characteristic, apparently, of the de Bleuchamps. But if the scar is not there, the white cat most assuredly is, just to enforce the continuity.

Blofeld's headquarters are in a remote part of the Swiss Alps, reachable only by helicopter. The shooting of the film, in fact, took place in a revolving restaurant newly built on the 3000 m (10,000 ft) high Schilthorn. (The film-makers offered to decorate the restaurant in exchange for permission to film there.)

The Piz Gloria, as it is known in the film, balances precariously on the edge of a steep drop. The whole location is a great excuse for a dynamic ski chase as Bond escapes from Blofeld's mountain stronghold. Arranged by John Glen (the action director of the second unit), the chase features a dramatic avalanche which was engineered by the Swiss army

using mortar bombs in an uninhabited part of the Alps. It was filmed by ski champion Willy Bogner who often used a hand-held camera even while skiing backwards to capture the scenes. John Jordan, back in the Bond team after his helicopter accident in *You Only Live Twice*, filmed from a helicopter above the action.

There is also, towards the end of the film, a fast-moving sled chase as Bond tries to apprehend Blofeld, but he escapes (by getting caught up in the branches of an overhanging tree) to take his revenge at the finish . . .

Irma Bunt

Blofeld's assistant, Fräulein Bunt, is a SPECTRE operative very much in the mould of *From Russia With Love*'s Rosa Klebb. The producers continued their successful policy of casting European stars, often in their first English-speaking role, by bringing in the German actress Ilse Steppat for the part. It is Bunt who controls the Institute with a rod of iron, making sure that rules are obeyed and that any fraternization between Bond/Bray and the girls is nipped in the bud. She is a pinched German matron who has clearly found her forte playing the tyrant over the girls.

Bond has, of course, found a way to beat the system and has been in the habit of sleeping with (among others) a young English girl – Ruby Violet from Morecambe Bay. It is in her room that he discovers the nightly whispered tapes which indoctrinate the girls with Blofeld's instructions for spreading his lethal spray. But one night, as he creeps into her bed, he finds himself confronted with Fräulein Bunt – a truly awful thought even for the amorous Bond – and his identity is out.

Blofeld (Telly Savalas) taunts 007 telling him that he has to learn to be absolutely calm before he can be let back into polite society.

The Bond Girl

Tracy

In *On Her Majesty's Secret Service* there is really only one girl for Bond (however much he sleeps around at the Institute). She is Teresa, Contessa di Vicenzo, but as she explains to Bond, 'Teresa was a saint, I'm known as Tracy'. Tracy was the girl trying to drown herself at the beach and once she is introduced to Bond their relationship develops and interweaves throughout the film – building up to the only occasion when 007 – as far as we know – genuinely falls in love.

As her father, Draco, tells Bond, while offering him £1 million to marry his daughter, she was spoiled as a child, had no real home, became caught up in a fast international set with one scandal following another and needs a man to help her settle down. Bond rejects his offer, preferring information about Blofeld to money; but in the end he falls for Tracy anyway – and without her father's financial encouragement.

Above *Draco (Gabriele Ferzetti) offers his daughter Tracy to Bond for £1 million. He believes that Bond might be a calming influence on her! However, Tracy turns out to have a very surprisng effect on Bond.*

Below *When M refuses to attack Blofeld's headquarters, Draco leads a squadron of fully-armed jet helicopters to storm the Piz Gloria at the summit of the snow-capped 3000 m (10,000 ft) Schilthorn.*

Tracy, played by Diana Rigg fresh from *The Avengers* TV series, is an unusually active Bond heroine. She can hold her own in most situations, driving her red Cougar with skill even when mixed up in a stock-car race; competing with Bond for expertise in the jumps, twists and turns of the ski chase; and joining in the fighting with her judo, defeating even the hefty hood Grunther. Her behaviour elicits the uncharacteristically admiring comment of 'good girl' from Bond on several occasions. Rigg, who is clearly used to this sort of thing in her adventures with *The Avengers'* Mr Steed, performed many of her stunts herself and, for once, the Bond girl makes quite an impact on the story.

Her father Draco is the head of the biggest crime syndicate in the West (excepting, of course, SPECTRE). Gabriele Ferzetti, former matinée idol and winner of two Italian film awards, plays the part with an aristocratic charm. Tracy and Draco get mixed up in the Blofeld business when she follows Bond to the Alps to pursue their relationship. Tracy is captured in the avalanche and as Blofeld holds the world to ransom, M (blithely unaware of the requirement that all Bond films end with the explosion of the villains' headquarters) refuses to take drastic action. So it is Draco's men and helicopters that are brought in to stage the climactic battle.

But that is not the end of the story, for *On Her Majesty's Secret Service* is essentially a romantic film. In a surprising finale, Tracy and Bond get married and there is a gentle, warm scene – almost out of place in a Bond film – where the wedding takes place with the full attendance of a fatherly M, a repentant Q and a tearful Miss Moneypenny.

The finale is more of an epilogue. Bond and Tracy are off on their honeymoon when they stop to remove some of the flowers on their car. Another car overtakes and there are gunshots; Bond thinks he recognizes Blofeld and turns to Tracy to tell her so. But Tracy is dead and Bond sits there, distraught, cradling her head, explaining to a passing policeman that they had, in Louis Armstrong's words, '. . . all the time in the world'.

So ends Bond's marriage and Lazenby's only stab at playing the dashing agent of the British Secret Service.

In a tragic ending to a romance, Bond discovers that his new bride Tracy has been killed by shots fired from Blofeld's passing car.

DOSSIER

007 ON HER MAJESTY'S SECRET SERVICE 1969 139 minutes

Producers
Harry Saltzman, Albert R. Broccoli
for Eon Productions

Director
Peter Hunt

Scriptwriter
Richard Maibaum

Director of photography
Michael Reed

Production designer
Syd Cain

Cameramen: 2nd Unit; aerial; ski
Egil Woxholt, Roy Ford; John Jordan;
Willy Bogner, Jr.. Alex Barbey

Special effects
John Stears

Stunt arranger; stock car sequence
George Leech; Anthony Squire

Editor and second unit director
John Glen

Main title designer
Maurice Binder

Music
composed, conducted and arranged
by John Barry

Song
'We Have All the Time in the World'
lyrics by Hal David
sung by Louis Armstrong

Distributor
United Artists

Cast includes
George Lazenby (James Bond)
Diana Rigg (Tracy)
Telly Savalas (Ernst Stavro Blofeld)
Gabriele Ferzetti (Draco)
Ilse Steppat (Irma Bunt)
Bernard Lee (M)
Angela Scoular (Ruby)
Lois Maxwell (Miss Moneypenny)
Catherina Von Schell (Bond girl no. 1)
George Baker (Sir Hilary Bray)
Desmond Llewelyn (Q)

Locations
filmed on location in Switzerland,
Portugal and at
Pinewood Studios, England

DIAMONDS ARE FOREVER

Sean Connery returns for one last time to play James Bond 007 and appears in what most people consider the wittiest Bond movie, famed for its wisecracking one-liners.

In many ways, *Diamonds Are Forever* was the turning point for the Bond films. Up until then there had been a continual tension between the almost ruthless machismo of the Fleming books and the fun-loving humorous romps of the films. Fleming's stories were hard-hitting and realistic: the films revelled in futuristic fantasy. Fleming's Bond was both steely and quietly ironic: in the films, 007 was always slightly self-mocking and his escapades more tongue-in-cheek. With *Diamonds Are Forever* the films crystallized into witty stylish adventures, and the plots bore remarkably little resemblance to their Fleming originals.

The team assembled for *Diamonds Are Forever* reflects the direction that the producers were taking. Peter Hunt had been replaced as director to try his hand elsewhere (he later moved into hard thrillers like *Death Hunt* and *Wild Geese 2*) and Guy Hamilton (who successfully combined Fleming and humour in *Goldfinger*) was back in the driving seat. Syd Cain, whose realistic sets graced *From Russia With Love* and *On Her Majesty's Secret Service*, was replaced by Ken Adam with his penchant for glittering futuristic designs. Richard Maibaum was brought back as the scriptwriter in addition to Tom Mankiewicz (father Joseph and uncle Herman wrote *Citizen Kane*) who had built a reputation on his way with one-liners.

To complete the package, Connery was made an offer he could not refuse. He was thought to have received $1 million (around £400,000 at the time) plus his picture fee which he donated to the Scottish Education Trust, a charity he had previously set up to help the educationally deprived in Scotland. In addition he is reputed to have been guaranteed a percentage of the profits, a £4000 (then around $10,000) per-week-over-schedule clause and a tacit agreement from United Artists to fund two films of his choice (Sidney Lumet's *The Offence* was made the following year). Although it was the last Connery Bond of the series, *Diamonds Are Forever* in fact sets the pattern for the Roger Moore Bonds of the Seventies.

The pre-title sequence demonstrates the transition. It starts violently with Bond accosting various people – including a girl whom he strangles with her own bikini top – to find Blofeld's location. (Yes, he's still chasing Blofeld who, after all, and as recently as *On Her Majesty's Secret Service*, had killed his wife!) But there the brutality ends and the fun begins. He traces his old adversary to a plastic surgery clinic, drowns the wrong man in a mudbath and then confronts the archvillain himself. In the ensuing skirmish, Blofeld lands in a pool of green slime which, when Bond throws the switch, starts to boil and Blofeld gurgles to death. As Blofeld commented on his entrance, 007 has been making mud pies and the fun continues in this vein throughout the film. The final shot of the sequence – a close-up of Blofeld's omnipresent white cat in a diamond-studded collar – is the only indication that things – or rather people – might not be quite what they seem.

The Assignment

M (who by this stage in the series can barely conceal his dislike of his star agent) introduces Bond to the problems of diamond smuggling. Despite apparent air-tight security at South Africa's diamond mines, a large quantity has recently gone missing. But more worrying than mere theft is the fact that none of the stolen jewels have found their way on to the world market. Bond is sent off to discover who is stockpiling the diamonds and why. He begins his mission by impersonating Franks, a dealer known to be part of the smuggling chain, and ends up in Las Vegas – face to face once more with Ernst Stavro Blofeld.

Blofeld has devised yet another way to hold the world to ransom. He has constructed a giant laser-beam generator suspended in orbit around the earth which uses the diamonds to intensify its energy to the point where it can cause rockets, missiles and submarines simply to self-detonate. Blofeld, in his element, is effectively conducting an international auction with nuclear supremacy going to the highest bidder.

Equipment Issued

Q's latest gadgets make themselves felt at several points in the film. Bond has false thumbprints to establish himself as Franks; he has a gun that shoots a rope out for climbing purposes (which he uses to ascend to Blofeld's penthouse, dangling dangerously over the dizzy heights of Las Vegas); and he

Left *James Bond tries his luck on a Las Vegas crap table while Plenty O'Toole (Lana Wood) waits to join his winnings.*

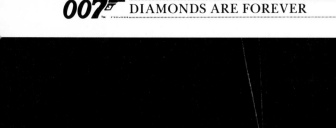

has a voice box for imitating other people's tones. Unfortunately, Blofeld also has one, which evens up the score somewhat. Q himself only surfaces in Las Vegas, far from his usual beat, enjoying himself (for once) playing fruit machines. He is apparently perfecting an electromagnetic device for getting all three symbols on the machine to line up. A useful gadget for any temporarily hard-up Secret Service agent!

Enemy Personnel

Ernst Stavro Blofeld

Top of the 'bad guys' list once again is Blofeld in positively his last appearance in the Bond series (apart from a cameo in *For Your Eyes Only*). To make up for his imminent disappearance, however, there are several of him. It seems that he has perfected a method of plastic surgery in order to make a series of duplicate Blofelds, the plan being to confuse his enemies and, in particular, Bond. (This, when discovered, explains how Bond appeared to kill Blofeld in the pre-title sequence but, in fact, did not.) When Bond is first confronted with two Blofelds he also spies the white cat. Thinking quickly he picks her up and throws her, landing a

Left *James Bond scales the heights of Willard Whyte's Las Vegas penthouse suite in order to find out who is running the diamond-smuggling operation.*

Below *Bond is confronted by two Blofelds – one on the sofa, one behind the desk. Only the white cat really knows which is the master and which is the clone – but who knows which is the real white cat?*

dart into the forehead of the Blofeld that she runs to. Just as he is complimenting himself on his ruse, another cat strolls into sight – this one is wearing the diamond-studded collar. 'Right idea', comments the real, very-much-alive Blofeld, 'But wrong pussy', answers Bond.

It turns out that Blofeld is holding millionaire recluse Willard Whyte hostage. No one has seen him for years – but thanks to Blofeld's voice-box impersonation they think they can still hear him, and so no one misses him. Blofeld has been using Whyte's vast network of resources for his own purposes.

This element of the plot arose from a dream of Broccoli's, which involved his friend, the millionaire recluse Howard Hughes, who had helped Broccoli establish himself at a crucial stage of his career. Broccoli used the scenario of his dream – namely, the kidnapping of Hughes and the use of his name by his would-be guardians to control his business – as a crucial component of the story of *Diamonds Are Forever*.

Blofeld is played by Charles Gray who had a bit-part as Henderson – our man on the spot – in *You Only Live Twice*. *Diamonds Are Forever* offered him his first major film role and he brought a convincing aristocratic veneer to the part of Blofeld. Building on this opportunity, he then established a career in television playing upper-class gentlemen (cads rather than villains) in various series.

Blofeld comes to a rather ambiguous end in *Diamonds Are Forever* – perhaps leaving the way open for further ransom threats in the future. He is last seen trying to escape from his oil-rig head-quarters in a personal capsule. But Bond has taken over the controls of the crane lowering him into the water, and he ends up being bounced up and down on the rig and generally used as a battering ram.

Mr Wint and Mr Kidd

Two professional hoods, Mr Wint and Mr Kidd, are (presumably on Blofeld's orders) killing off all the human links in the diamond-smuggling chain. They have a close relationship – homosexuality is hinted at when they walk off hand in hand, after one killing, into the sunset – and a neat line in repartee, rivalling Bond's own, as they roam around the film like the prototypes of the buddy-buddy American outlaws. On one occasion while contemplating a scorpion about to be put to a deadly purpose, Wint comments, 'One of nature's finest experts, Mr Kidd'. 'One is never too old to learn from a true professional, Mr Wint', the other replies. But their best exchange is reserved – natur-ally – for Bond who is trapped in a coffin which is slowly heading for the crematorium fire. 'Heart-

Above *Charles Gray was the last actor to play Blofeld in the James Bond 007 series.*

Below *Mr Kidd (Putter Smith), one half of a back-chatting, murderous pair of hoods, suffers a fiery end when Bond poors brandy on his flaming kebabs.*

'warming', says one. 'A glowing tribute', replies the other. *Diamonds Are Forever* is unique among Bond films in that the villains have the wittier lines. In the nick of time, 007 is rescued from a fiery death by his would-be assassins who discover that the diamonds he has passed on to them are fake.

Wint and Kidd meet a fitting end in the epilogue to the film. Bond and Tiffany (a diamond crook turned Bond-helper) are celebrating their victory over Blofeld by returning to England on a cruise ship. Two waiters enter to serve them their dinner. With the aid of one waiter's ignorance of wines (never a way to fool 007) and the other's memorably pungent aftershave, Bond recognizes the pair as Wint and Kidd. A fight ensues in which Kidd ends up in flames and jumps overboard to extinguish the

fire. Wint follows him, having had his dinner jacket tied up around his legs like a diaper and his own bomb, disguised as a luscious dessert, fixed to it. 'He left with his tails between his legs', says Bond, eliciting the last laugh.

Bambi and Thumper

The final duo of Blofeld's team are Bambi and Thumper, whose names are a cheeky tip of the hat to Walt Disney from the producers. These two delightfully back-flipping, high-kicking girls have the task of guarding the millionaire Whyte. Played by two acrobats, Donna Garrett and Trina Parks, the pair engage Bond in one of the most entertaining fights of the series.

Above left *James Bond triumphs over his final would-be assassin of the film, Mr Wint (Bruce Glover) – who seems to be relishing the experience.*

Left *Bambi (Donna Garrett) and Thumper (Trina Parks) demonstrate they are less cuddly than their namesakes when they throw Bond into a pool to prevent him finding the whereabouts of Willard Whyte.*

The Bond Girl

Tiffany Case

So named when her mother gave birth in the famous New York jewellers while looking for a wedding ring, Tiffany Case is a vivacious red-haired woman who is one of the key links in the diamond chain. She drives a red Mustang which becomes involved in the most exciting car chase in the film when Bond and Tiffany escape from the Las Vegas police, smashing up and jumping over cars in a crowded parking lot and finally driving the Mustang on its side through a narrow alleyway.

The Ford Motor Company who provided all the cars for this sequence were surprised at just how many of their vehicles had to be written off after the Bond team had finished with them. The chase contains a glaring continuity error – remarkable for the fact that it is hardly ever noticed. When the Mustang tilts on its side, it is first seen driving on only its left wheels, but by the end of the sequence, it is driving on the right pair. The stunt itself is so daring that no one sees the mistake.

Tiffany is something of a good-time girl – first allying herself to one side, then to another, according to which way she sees her bread buttered. But one glance at Wint and Kidd and their murderous activities (as opposed to Bond's invincible charm) convinces her to return to the straight and narrow. It is just at this point, however, that she is captured by Blofeld and taken to his oil-rig head-quarters. When Bond finally arrives to rescue her – and Western civilization – there are a few farcical mix-ups before they both escape into a waiting boat seconds before the inevitable explosion.

Jill St John gives a lightheartedly dizzy perform-ance as Tiffany, combining cunning and allure to make her just a little more than dumb. After several similar roles in films she went into business, thus belying her usual casting as a dumb broad. She returned to the screen in the Eighties to appear as a TV cook on *Good Morning, America*.

The Victim

Plenty O'Toole

'I'm Plenty', is how a girl at the casino introduces herself to Bond. 'I bet you are', he replies. 'Plenty O'Toole', she continues. 'Named after your father?', he enquires. Plenty, played by Lana Wood (forever being labelled Natalie's sister) is a dark gregarious gambler who wanders in and out of the story, trying to woo the available Bond. Her exits are particularly notable: the first time, she leaves Bond's bedroom by the window – thrown down several storeys by a hood to land in a handy swimming pool. 'Good shot', comments Bond. 'I didn't know it was there', mumbles the hood. (The hood, incidentally, is played by famous Hollywood gangster actor Marc Lawrence who reappears in the opening sequence of *The Man With the Golden Gun*). Next time she is not so lucky and is found floating face down in Tiffany's swimming pool.

Above left *In Bond's hands, Tiffany's red Mustang can drive through even the narrowest alleyways. (Watch the film carefully to see which way the car is tilting when it drives into the alley!)*

Left *Tiffany Case (Jill St John) 'showing a bit more cheek than usual' as she tries to replace the cassette that programs Blofeld's computer.*

The Background Story

Diamonds Are Forever is memorable both for its witty one-liners and its occasional, almost surreal, elements. At one point they are combined. Bond, in his role as Franks, is smuggling the diamonds into the USA in a coffin. He is met at customs by his old colleague Felix Leiter (here played by Norman Burton). Leiter examines the coffin and the corpse but can see no sign of the stolen jewels. 'Alimentary, my dear Leiter', comments Bond.

When Bond infiltrates Whyte's factory to try and trace the diamonds he becomes entangled in an astronaut's simulation exercise, escaping from the place by a moon buggy. This leads to one of the most bizarre chases to date as Bond in the buggy lumbers across the desert outside the factory chased by guards in bikes specially adapted for travelling over sand dunes. It is a quite extraordinary scene which provides a typical topical reference point – Apollo 15, launched in the year of the film's release,

was the first moon mission to use the famous Lunar Roving Vehicle.

Towards the end of the film, there is one more surreal moment – when Bond is parachuted down to the ocean near Blofeld's headquarters. He approaches the oil rig inside a giant silver ball which bounces across the water to his destination. In fact, there was a pedal bike inside the ball which allowed the occupant to propel it forwards. It is touches such as these that make *Diamonds Are Forever* a very memorable Bond movie.

Right *Blofeld's headquarters, from which he can direct the giant laser generator in the sky, are situated on an oil rig. For the film, the chosen location was a rig off-shore from Oceanside in California.*

Below *Bond finds himself in a classified security area of the Willard Whyte plant, where equipment for the US space shot is being prepared. It provides a bizarre backdrop for an unusual Bond chase which involves the moon buggy (seen here) and specially adapted lunar bikes.*

007 DIAMONDS ARE FOREVER 1971 119 minutes

Producers
Harry Saltzman, Albert R. Broccoli
for Eon Productions

Director
Guy Hamilton

Scriptwriters
Richard Maibaum, Tom Mankiewicz

Director of photography
Ted Moore

Production designer
Ken Adam

Special effects
Leslie Hillman, Whitey McMahon

Stunt arrangers
Bob Simmons, Paul Baxley

Sound
Gordon McCallum, John Mitchell,
Alfred J. Overton
(Academy Award nomination)

Editors
Bert Bates, John W. Holmes

Main title designer
Maurice Binder

Music
composed, conducted and arranged
by John Barry

Title song
lyrics by Don Black,
sung by Shirley Bassey

Distributor
United Artists

Cast includes
Sean Connery (James Bond)
Jill St John (Tiffany Case)
Charles Gray (Ernst Stavro Blofeld)
Lana Wood (Plenty O'Toole)
Jimmy Dean (Willard Whyte)
Bruce Cabot (Saxby)
Bernard Lee (M)
Lois Maxwell (Miss Moneypenny)
Putter Smith (Mr Kidd)
Bruce Glover (Mr Wint)
Marc Lawrence (gangster)
Desmond Llewelyn (Q)

Locations
filmed on location in USA,
Germany, the Netherlands, France
and at Pinewood Studios, England

LIVE AND LET DIE

Like Sean Connery, Roger Moore started his career as James Bond on location in Jamaica for this encounter with voodoo, superstition and the drug trade.

This is very much a film of the Seventies – both in plot and in style. Its story revolves around the world trade in heroin from its growth in San Monique, a small fictitious island in the Caribbean, to its distribution in Harlem. (At the time that Fleming wrote the novel, he would never have thought to include hard drugs in his books.)

The black mafia behind the heroin traffic is also very much a product of the Seventies. At this time, films like *Shaft* and *Superfly* had brought black actors into the limelight and *Live and Let Die* makes use of some of these new stars.

With Connery's departure from the Bond series, Roger Moore is now immersed in the coveted role. Moore had made a name for himself in TV series like *The Saint* and *The Persuaders* as a suave and sophisticated action man who has a way with the ladies – so the transition to Bond was not too painful. In addition, he excelled at light comedy, reinforcing the direction that the films were already taking.

The combination of these two elements made *Live and Let Die* a fast-paced, hard thriller with Bond himself playing the light relief. Indeed in the tarot-card motif which recurs throughout the film, Bond, in an amusing in-joke, is initially represented by The Fool (later, this changes, and Bond becomes one of The Lovers). The new 007, with his lighter touch and wittier approach, had clearly surfaced.

The film-makers were so confident that Moore would be acceptable to the public as Bond that not one of the tricks to introduce Lazenby to the audience was used. In fact, Bond does not even appear until after the pre-title sequence which sets the stage for the events to follow with three killings in rapid succession. The first occurs at an international conference in New York where the British representative is buzzed to death through his earphones. The second takes place in New Orleans in a memorable scene in which a spectator at a black funeral finds the coffin in the procession is his own. When he is safely inside it – dead – the band changes from playing a dirge to an up-beat jazz rhythm and the mourners start to dance. The third victim is bitten by a poisonous snake in a voodoo ceremony in San Monique.

Left *Roger Moore made his debut as Ian Fleming's famed agent in* Live and Let Die. *He went on to play the role in seven films in the series.*

The Assignment

For once, M – with Miss Moneypenny in tow – visits Bond at his apartment (not the same one, incidentally, as that seen in *Dr No*). They interrupt his latest amour to issue instructions. Three agents (the victims of the pre-title sequence) have been killed in the last 24 hours and Bond's task is to find out if they are connected.

His search takes him first to Harlem where a very white Bond sticks out like a sore thumb. He is kidnapped by Mr Big when visiting the Fillet of Soul restaurant after half of Harlem has phoned in his whereabouts. ('You can't miss him – it's like following a cue ball.') From there he goes to San Monique where he discovers that Dr Kananga is growing fields of poppies under camouflaged netting. Finally, he lands in New Orleans (where the heroin is processed) to learn that Mr Big and Dr Kananga are one and the same person and that he intends to distribute two tons of free heroin as a move to control the US market for his organization.

Equipment Issued

While Q himself is not actually present in this film, his influence is surely felt. He has mended Bond's watch – a nifty time-piece (first introduced in this film and used at several points in it) which can be turned into a powerful magnet at the press of a button (it also has another trick which is not revealed until later). When M and Miss Moneypenny are safely out of the way, Bond promptly demonstrates its use as a magnet on the zip of his girlfriend's dress. Other gadgets which appear include the usual bug detectors, a transmitter disguised as a shaving brush and a shark gun which uses compressed air pellets.

Enemy Personnel

Mr Big and Dr Kananga

The brains behind the Harlem underworld is Mr Big ('You name the business, they say he has the black concession'), while Dr Kananga, the Prime Minister of San Monique, makes his presence felt at international conferences. They are both busy and powerful men. When Bond makes a fool of himself in Harlem, Mr Big only interrupts his business long enough to order 'Kill the honky'. In San Monique,

Dr Kananga only takes a moment from more pressing affairs to issue instructions to kill 007. In this aim they are clearly united. In Harlem, Mr Big runs the show with the aid of a network of hoods – as they say, there is but one man in Harlem who can pull that kind of muscle. Dr Kananga in San Monique, on the other hand, uses voodoo and superstition, skulls and ritual to protect his operation. Solitaire, the tarot-card reader, accompanies both men everywhere – and indeed, they are the same person.

Yaphet Kotto, who plays the dual role, is one of the black actors who came to prominence in the Seventies, even starting his own company, New Era Productions, to open doors for the ethnic minorities in Hollywood. He has continued to get good parts in movies, appearing in films like *Raid on Entebbe* (he played Idi Amin), *Blue Collar*, *Brubaker* and *Alien*. He is an actor of note and his versatility is clearly evident in *Live and Let Die*.

Like all villains in Bond movies, Dr Kananga comes to a sticky end – albeit, in this case, an ignoble one. Having bombed Kananga's poppy fields, Bond, with Solitaire, is trapped in his underground headquarters. Kananga has them tied to a pulley which will be slowly lowered into a nearby pool of sharks (after he has cut Bond's wrist to produce blood to alert the flesh-eaters). Bond uses his watch to attract the casing of a compressed air pellet, then presses another button on the versatile watch which turns it into a buzz-saw and cuts them both free. In the ensuing fight, Bond pops the pellet into Kananga's mouth; he then expands and expands until he explodes with a bang.

Tee Hee

Mr Big's henchman in Harlem is Tee Hee, a thin-faced hood with a metal hook for an arm which he can turn into an awesome weapon. (Bond learns later that the original limb was chewed off by an alligator.) Tee Hee's most ingenious method of disposing of 007 occurs at a crocodile farm (where the heroin is processed). Its entrance is guarded with the immortal words 'Trespassers Will Be Eaten'. Tee Hee and Bond walk onto a bridge to feed the crocodiles and alligators, but part of it retracts leaving Bond stranded on an island in the middle of hundreds of hungry reptiles. First Bond tries to use the magnetic watch to attract a nearby boat, but it is firmly moored. Then, with no Q-designed gadget left to help him, he solves his problem in truly spectacular Bond fashion – by using a row of crocs as stepping-stones to get to the shore.

The stunt was performed at an actual crocodile farm owned (by coincidence) by a Ross Kananga.

His Swamp Safari in Jamaica is a tourist attraction covering 120 hectares (300 acres) and containing some 1500 crocodiles (and alligators). In fact, it was Kananga who performed the dangerous stepping-stone stunt across the crocodiles who had their heads and legs tied down under the water and out of sight. It is a superb moment that epitomizes the daring combination of humour and thrills which

makes the James Bond 007 films so popular.

Tee Hee (like Red Grant in *From Russia With Love*) gets his comeuppance on a train. In an echo of the earlier fight, Tee Hee slogs it out with Bond. Finally the resourceful British agent spies a pair of nail-cutters and snips the steel cables of the villain's metal arm as a prelude to throwing him out of the window.

Left *Bond uses his ingenuity to keep the lethal steel arm of Tee Hee (Julius Harris) at bay.*

Below *Solitaire (Jane Seymour) has betrayed Dr Kananga and ruined her talent for seeing the future; her punishment is to be introduced to a poisonous reptile from the San Monique jungle.*

Baron Samedi

Dr Kananga's aide in San Monique is the mysterious Baron Samedi, played by Geoffrey Holder, a 2 m (6 ft 6 in) tall dancer. Holder, who has his own dance company in New York, also choreographed the voodoo dances. With his white-and-black-painted face, Baron Samedi is a traditional symbol of Death in voodoo culture and is represented by a skull in the tarot pack.

At first, he has only a shadowy presence – first seen in a tourist show, now sitting on a grave playing a pipe, then advising Dr Kananga. His more fore-boding appearance is during a voodoo ritual where the mesmerized dancers are celebrating the approaching death of Solitaire by snake-bite. The participants summon him by knocking on a grave-stone three times. He rises from the ground and Bond shoots – only to find it is a hollow façade. He rises again, this time to be thrown by Bond into a coffin full of writhing snakes. But Death cannot himself be killed and at the end of the film, when Bond and Solitaire are riding into the sunset, he can be seen – complete with eerie laugh – sitting on the rear platform of their train. It is an unusual Bond ending but one which neatly ties up the tarot-card theme of the film.

The Bond Girl

Solitaire

The High Priestess of the tarot deck is clearly the card that symbolizes Solitaire. She has inherited the gift of second sight, describing her calling as, 'wife to the prince no longer of this world, the spiritual bridge into the secret church'. Whether anyone believes this or not, she certainly has a useful knack of predicting the future. She knows it is a heavenly gift which, if violated by earthly love (ie, sex), can be taken away. Kananga knows this and values her clairvoyant powers; he is, therefore, 'saving her' for a later date. Bond, however, is blithely unaware of the consequences of seducing her, and when the cards continually reveal Solitaire and Bond to be The Lovers he succumbs to their wish and ruins Solitaire in more ways than one.

Solitaire spends most of the film alternately escaping from and being caught by Kananga. After Bond has seduced her (with the aid of a tarot pack consisting solely of The Lovers), they manage to depart from San Monique on Quarrel Junior's fishing boat (Quarrel Junior is the son of Bond's assistant in *Dr No*), but are trapped by Kananga's men at New Orleans airport. Kananga discovers that Solitaire has lost her powers and she becomes the intended victim of another voodoo rite, only to be rescued in the nick of time by the resourceful

Bond. Their escape (via Baron Samedi's grave) leads them into Kananga's hands, once again. This time he tries to eliminate the pair by feeding them to the sharks but, yet again, his plans go wrong.

With her long brown hair and soft-spoken, very correct English tones, Jane Seymour is right for the part, sitting there turning the cards with proper decorum and speaking her prophecies in dulcet monotones. Seymour had originally trained as a ballet dancer but had to abandon this career when she developed cartilage trouble. The producers spotted her when she was in a TV series *The Onedin Line*. She came to the audition with her hat on. When she removed it, her long flowing hair spilled out beautifully from under it making an immediate impact on the producers. She has been a regular fixture in TV sagas such as the British *The Winds of War* and Australia's *East of Eden* ever since.

Dr Kananga (Yaphet Kotto) prepares Bond and Solitaire for a watery grave. He is about to lower them into his shark pool, having first taken the precaution of cutting Bond's wrist to encourage the flesheaters' appetites.

The Victim

Rosie Carver

Represented in the tarot pack by the Queen of Cups (a lying and deceitful woman), Rosie Carver arrives in San Monique calling herself Mrs Bond. She is the local CIA agent on only her second mission. Actress Gloria Hendry, with her vivacious presence, is a complete contrast to Jane Seymour's restrained Solitaire. Hendry, like many another Bond-movie girl, is a veteran of beauty contests but it was while working as a Playboy Bunny that director Daniel Mann discovered her and offered her a part in *For the Love of Ivy*. She went on to appear in many of the black movies of the Seventies.

With her inexperience, bumbling manner and tendency to make mistakes, Rosie is a likeable character and it is something of a disappointment to discover that she is really in the pay of Kananga. Like Quarrel in *Dr No*, Rosie is superstitious – she especially fears the skull-like scarecrows that adorn Kananga's estate. In a sequence that echoes Quarrel's death in *Dr No* (he, remember, fell victim to a 'dragon' of a tank), she is killed, when her double game has outlasted its usefulness to Kananga, by a scarecrow with two guns protruding through its eyes.

At this point in the story it is not clear whose side Rosie Carver (Gloria Hendry) is on. She could be working for Dr Kananga or she could be Bond's San Monique contact. James Bond is clearly trying to find out in the way that he knows best.

The Background Story

Live and Let Die is memorable for its stunts which grace the film at various stages. Long before hang-gliding became a trendy sport, Bond uses an 18 kg (40 lb) kite, flying 250 m (800 ft) high to scout Kananga's land from the air. Glider expert Bill Bennot designed the kite himself and flew it for the film. It is a nice touch aided by some competent aerial photography.

Later in the film, when Bond and Solitaire are escaping from Kananga's men, they find a double-decker bus in a village. The ensuing chase climaxes when Bond drives the bus under a low bridge, cutting off the top deck which promptly falls on top of the following car. It is a well-executed stunt which needed the involvement of London bus-driving instructor Maurice Patchett who taught Moore to drive the vehicle as well as advising on the crash itself.

James Bond finds another exotic way of travelling by air. His hang-glider can fly 250 m (800 ft) above the sea and cliffs for a distance of 3 km (2 miles); thus he is able to float down silently and surprise one of Kananga's guards.

One of the best stunts in Live and Let Die *occurs when Solitaire and Bond are escaping from Dr Kananga. They appropriate a double-decker bus only to find their way barred by a low-level bridge which neatly slices off the top deck – which falls on top of the pursuing car. The stunt was arranged by cutting the bus in half before shooting the scene, and resting the top piece on rollers so that when the bus hit the bridge the upper deck could easily sheer off.*

Below *A Glastron speedboat is jumped over the highway between two sections of the bayou. The boat was equipped with an Evinrude Starflite 135 hp motor and was streamlined by moving all its weight towards the centre so that it could leap a distance of 30 m (95 ft) and a height of 4 m (13 ft).*

Bottom *A wedding in the gardens of a plantation is disturbed by the arrival of 007 in his speedboat trying to find a shortcut between waterways. The groom was played by the son of the plantation owner – William Treadway II – who allowed the Bond team to film in his grounds.*

But undoubtedly the highlight of this film is the lengthy speedboat chase across the Louisiana bayou country. While red-neck Sheriff Pepper (played by character actor Clifton James and destined to reappear in *The Man With the Golden Gun*) is tearing his hair out at the havoc being created throughout his county, speedboats are crashing into trees, smashing into wedding cakes, colliding with police cars and making the most spectacular jumps imaginable across roads. Some 13 high-powered aquajets and a further 13 150-hp speedboats were used for these scenes and all kinds of ramps and structures had to be erected to create the right effects. The humour arising from the character of Sheriff Pepper, combined with the top-gear thrills of the stunts themselves, make this the kind of chase sequence for which the Bond films are rightly famous.

Left *Bond's pursuer lands his flying speedboat slap in the middle of a police car – forcing Sheriff Pepper (Clifton James) to realize that he will never catch the lunatics on the loose in his territory.*

Below *At the end of the film, Baron Samedi (Geoffrey Holder) is perched mockingly on the rear of the train taking Bond and Solitaire home, knowing that victory is his. Baron Samedi is a symbol of immense magical powers in voodoo and, like Death, he cannot be killed.*

DOSSIER

007 LIVE AND LET DIE 1973 121 minutes

Producers
Harry Saltzman, Albert R. Broccoli
for Eon Productions

Director
Guy Hamilton

Scriptwriter
Tom Mankiewicz

Director of photography
Ted Moore

Supervising art director
Syd Cain

Special effects
Derek Meddings

Stunt coordinators
Bob Simmons, Joie Chitwood,
Ross Kananga, Jerry Comeaux,
Eddie Smith, Bill Bennet

Editors
Bert Bates, Raymond Poulton,
John Shirley

Main title designer
Maurice Binder

Music
score by George Martin

Title song
by Paul and Linda McCartney,
sung and performed by
Paul McCartney and Wings
(Academy Award nomination)

Distributor
United Artists

Cast includes
Roger Moore (James Bond)
Yaphet Kotto (Dr Kananga/Mr Big)
Jane Seymour (Solitaire)
Clifton James (Sheriff Pepper)
Julius W. Harris (Tee Hee)
Geoffrey Holder (Baron Samedi)
David Hedison (Felix Leiter)
Gloria Hendry (Rosie Carver)
Bernard Lee (M)
Lois Maxwell (Miss Moneypenny)
Roy Stewart (Quarrel Junior)

Locations
filmed on location in USA, Jamaica
and at Pinewood Studios, England

THE MAN WITH THE GOLDEN GUN

The ninth Bond movie takes 007 to the most exotic location to date –
the colourful locales of the Far East.

The ninth film in the Bond series, based very loosely on Fleming's novel, begins and ends with a game – a deadly cat-and-mouse chase through a weird maze. It is a device which serves as a guide to the plot of the film as a whole, with its various meanderings through multiple twists and turns among the exotic locations of the Far East. It is never even clear quite who is the cat and who is the mouse as Bond searches for Scaramanga, the man with the golden gun. He, in turn, is out to kill his greatest rival – James Bond.

The pre-title sequence is set on Scaramanga's island, somewhere off the coast of China. With its volcanic rocky outcrops and sandy beaches, it is a strange and unusual location which adds a weird flavour to the proceedings. A hood (played by Marc Lawrence who previously appeared in *Diamonds Are Forever*) arrives to collect a pay-off and the scenery becomes even odder as Scaramanga lures him to play out his murderous game in his specially designed fun room. The fun room (created by production designer Peter Murton who had worked as an art director on previous Bond movies) uses optical illusions, mirrors and coloured lights to spin a web of confusion.

The entrant to the maze must work his way through Wild West saloons, shooting galleries and fairground booths, and past distorting mirrors to face armed (and shooting) waxwork dummies and various other hazards. In the fun room it is very definitely a case of kill or be killed. The whole game is orchestrated by the diminutive Nick Nack who shouts encouragement and advice while manipulating the levers and switches of the game. Of course, Scaramanga wins, neatly disposing of the hood with one deadly accurate shot from his golden gun. He then turns to blow the top off a nearby figure – a life-like cut-out of James Bond.

The Assignment

Bond is taken off his current assignment – the search for a missing solar-energy scientist – when a golden bullet engraved with the figures 007 arrives at headquarters. M takes this as an indication that Scaramanga, the highest-paid assassin in the business, has got Bond's number. Bond is ordered to resign and lie low – or hunt out Scaramanga himself – before he can resume active service. He has one lead – the death of agent 002 in 1969, rumoured to have been shot with a golden bullet.

Bond's search takes him to Beirut (where he locates the spent golden bullet ornamenting the belly of a dancer); to a gun-maker in Macao (which leads to the best line in the film as Bond aims a gun at his groin with the command, 'Speak now or

Left *It is hard to tell which is more deadly – Francisco Scaramanga (Christopher Lee) or his notorious golden gun.*

Right *Distorted images confuse Bond when he confronts a reflection of Scaramanga in his cunningly constructed fun room.*

Left *A high-level conference aboard the sunken liner in Hong Kong harbour as Bond meets up with his boss M (Bernard Lee), Hip (Soon-Taik Oh) and the omnipresent Q (Desmond Llewelyn).*

forever hold your piece'); and to Hong Kong where he makes contact with Scaramanga's mistress Andrea Anders.

From here on things become steadily more complex. For when Bond finally crosses paths with the man with the golden gun – in fact, Scaramanga has 007 clearly in his sights – it is not Bond who is the victim of his target practice but the missing solar energy scientist. When Bond makes contact with M, quartered in the wreck of the *Queen Elizabeth* in Hong Kong harbour, things become clearer. The scientist, who has developed a device known as a solex – a pocket-sized solar agitator which is capable of converting radiation from the sun into pure energy – had decided to defect to the East. He was on his way home again when he met his death. Scaramanga, it seems, is after the solex for his own purposes and so for the rest of the film, Bond's two missions are inextricably linked.

Equipment Issued

Q is somewhat upstaged this time around by Scaramanga who has all the best gadgets himself. Q's only contribution to Bond's welfare is to supply him with a fake third nipple (Scaramanga's distinguishing mark). In fact, Q seems to get on his colleagues' nerves as he tirelessly explains the science behind yet another device, looking and acting more like an absent-minded professor with each film.

Q does come up trumps, however, in analyzing the origins of the golden bullet – it is made from soft 23-carat gold with traces of nickel and (as Q patiently explains to Bond) could only have been fashioned by a Portuguese gun-maker living in Macao. Meanwhile, in the background of Q's lab, an elaborate visual joke is going on. A new apparatus is being tested and careful measurements are being taken to pinpoint its exact range and impact. When the machine finally does fire, it blows a large hole in the target wall, thus making a mess of the scientists' precise work. It is clearly a case of 'back to the drawing board'.

Enemy Personnel

Francisco Scaramanga

'The man with the golden gun' is the world's number one hired assassin, commanding a fee of $1 million a hit. He has his own gun, which can be assembled from a cigarette case, a lighter, a cufflink and a pen (made by Colibri Lighters from the film's design of the gun) and always uses a golden bullet to make his mark. He has an abnormality, a third nipple, which is apparently considered a sign of invulnerability and sexual prowess. In the film, though, it is considered a sign for a plethora of ripe puns – ' a fascinating anatomical titbit', 'he must have found me quite titillating', and so on.

Scaramanga delights in gadgetry. Apart from his do-it-yourself gun, he has a car which can sprout wings and become an airplane. (When Q hears of it, he boasts that he was just working on a similar project.) The look on the spectators' faces (who include Sheriff Pepper imported from *Live and Let Die*) when the car takes to the air is a moment of pure farce.

Scaramanga is played by the veteran star of horror movies, Christopher Lee. Ironically, Lee and Moore started in films together with small parts in *Trottie True*, 25 years earlier. Just as his Dracula is an aristocratic killer, so his Scaramanga is a suave, cultured man who uses his ill-gotten gains to live the kind of good life that Bond himself might envy. His island has every type of modern convenience making the place a kind of isolated paradise. He also has the sought-after solex, which not only supplies an unlimited amount of power for his retreats but also channels energy towards more deadly ends – such as blowing up Bond's plane.

As Bond recalls, Scaramanga was born in a circus, the son of the ring-master (probably Cuban) and the snake-charmer (English). He was a spectacular trick-shot artist by the time he was ten and a gunman by the age of fifteen. He was recruited by the KGB as an overworked and underpaid assassin but went independent in the late Fifties to reap the fruit of his own efforts.

Later in the films he tells Bond, in a rare moment of confidence, how he became a killer when the circus keeper shot his best friend – a magnificent African bull elephant. Scaramanga killed the keeper and had not looked back since. He is fond of drawing analogies (which infuriate Bond) between his own and 007's work, arguing that, as killers, they belong to the same breed. All of which makes Scaramanga a rather endearing character and Lee portrays him with more sympathy than many Bond villains have been shown.

He meets his match, however, when he challenges 007 to a duel. For when it is Bond's turn to engage in a showdown among the tricks and twists of the fun room, he breaks out of the maze and wins the game by the cunning device of disguising himself as his own cardboard cut-out.

Above *This is the kind of ingenious device that even Q might envy. With Nick Nack (Hervé Villechaize) as passenger, Scaramanga drives an American Motors Coupe that sprouts wings and transforms itself into an airplane. Hidden in the trunk is Mary Goodnight, an accident-prone young lady whose help poses Bond with nearly as many problems as does Scaramanga.*

Left *Who is out to kill whom? Bond may have met his match in this duel with the man whose deadly accuracy has earned him the title of 'man with the golden gun'.*

Nick Nack

At just over 1 m (3 ft 10 in) Nick Nack is by far the smallest henchman of a Bond movie. Despite his size, French actor Hervé Villechaize is in constant demand whenever an appropriate stage or screen role appears. After his success in *The Man With the Golden Gun* he was noticed by Hollywood and cast in the TV series *Fantasy Island*.

As Nick Nack, with thick black hair and impish features (at one point he is able to disguise himself as a garden gnome), he chatters away with an accented lilt making him quite unlike other Bond villains. Apart from being Scaramanga's general factotum (including a cordon bleu chef), his main role is as the master of ceremonies of the game. It is Nick Nack who sets the game up, manipulates the controls and keeps up an informative monologue about its progress. But he is also Scaramanga's heir – which adds an extra spicy twist to the outcome of the game.

As is the way with loyal henchmen in Bond movies, Nick Nack is still out for blood even when his master has cashed in his chips. So after the final explosion, when Bond and his girlfriend, Mary Goodnight, are on Scaramanga's junk returning to Hong Kong, Nick Nack turns up with murder in his eyes. After a baffling fight – 007 is not used to opponents who hide under beds or kick his ankles (despite Rosa Klebb's poisoned toe-caps in *From Russia With Love*) – Bond finally finds the answer. He shuts Nick Nack in a suitcase and fixes him to the sails of the junk as a kind of masthead.

Above *Mary Goodnight (Britt Ekland) tries to help Bond retrieve the solex. But would anyone in their right mind allow the hamfisted Goodnight to play with the controls when as a result anything could go wrong?*

Left *A small interruption to Bond's romance! Nick Nack disturbs 007's amorous finalé with Goodnight.*

Left *Mary Goodnight has done it again. Leaning against the controls she releases a burst of energy which nearly frazzles Bond.*

Below *Francisco Scaramanga using his golden gun to persuade his mistress Andrea (Maud Adams) to follow his orders.*

The Bond Girl

Mary Goodnight

The British Secret Service agent for Thailand is Goodnight, a young lady who has clearly had a fling with 007 in London and is hoping for more of the same. However, like Sylvia Trench in *Dr No*, Mary Goodnight finds her intentions badly thwarted. In fact, she has a rather uncomfortable time, getting herself crammed into wardrobes or imprisoned in the trunk of a car. She also has a tendency to make a mess of things, yet Swedish actress Britt Ekland manages to rescue her from being merely a dumb blonde with nice touches of humour.

Her best string of mistakes starts when she ends up in the trunk of Scaramanga's car and is taken to his island. While Bond disposes of Scaramanga, Goodnight tackles the lone maintenance engineer but unfortunately dumps him into one of the cooling vats associated with the solar-energy complex. This triggers the inevitable countdown to the explosion – but Bond still has to disentangle the solex from the apparatus to return it to HQ. With the hamfisted Goodnight at the controls, Bond has a difficult job and nearly gets burnt alive when Goodnight's posterior backs into the wrong button. The pair retrieve the device and escape the island just before it finally blows.

Now safely on the junk, having tied up Nick Nack, they can finally indulge their pleasure – only to find themselves interrupted by M on the telephone. But Bond leaves him on the hook, plaintively calling for Goodnight. 'Goodnight, sir', says Bond and puts the phone down.

The Victim

Andrea Anders

Swedish cover girl Maud Adams plays Andrea, Scaramanga's frustrated mistress. Her distress arises because Scaramanga pays her attention only immediately before a job. She consoles herself by fluttering her eyelashes at Bond in order to convince him to kill her lover. It turns out that it was Andrea, with just this aim in mind, who had sent the golden bullet to M in the first place. But once Scaramanga discovers her treachery, it is her name that is on one of his deadly bullets. When Bond has a date with her in a Thai boxing stadium, he sits down to have a chat before he realizes that Andrea, sitting next to him, has already been shot. Maud Adams reappears in the title role of *Octopussy*, nearly a decade after *The Man With the Golden Gun*.

The Background Story

All the key elements of the Bond movies are present in *The Man With the Golden Gun*. There are the exotic locations, with the clubs, dancers, streets and vessels of Macao, Hong Kong and Bangkok. There are the memorable sets, chief of which is the sloping, angular structure of the Hong Kong Secret Service headquarters located inside the half-sunk wreck of the *Queen Elizabeth* liner in Hong Kong harbour. There is a marvellous spoof in a martial-arts school where Bond has been taken to be finished off. Though every action is accompanied by measured bows and polite ritual, made famous by the contemporary trend of Kung Fu movies, the karate experts are out for the kill. They are stopped, not by Bond – who despite his expertise in the martial arts, is outnumbered – but by two schoolgirls who dispose of the black belts in a few easy minutes. The idea for this sequence arose when schoolgirl Joie Pacharin-Traporn, who was a black belt in karate, having studied it for seven years, wrote to the producers asking to be part of the film. They complied, resulting in an amusingly conceived sequence.

The location for Scaramanga's headquarters was found in the remote village of Pang Na near the beautiful Thai resort of Phukett. According to Charles (Jerry) Juroe, the head of marketing for Eon Productions, Pang Na is 'generally conceded by Bond veterans to be the most physically difficult of any of the Bond locations'. Even the best rooms in the unit's hotel had extremely primitive facilities – and those were for the stars!

As if the conditions were not difficult enough, there were also hazards getting to the island where the unit was filming . The journey passed a village

Above *An American Motors Hornet Hatchback rolls over in a mid-air leap while crossing a river. This spectacular stunt took months of precise calculations on a Hal 2000 computer to design. When it was performed it was over in two seconds, and was captured on film in one take.*

Left *Bond is outclassed by the pupils of a martial arts school. But two young schoolgirls come to the rescue, throwing, kicking and chopping the parts that Bond could not reach.*

on stilts, traditionally inhabited by pirates who originally came from Indonesia and, even today, passersby are expected to pay tribute to the villagers. Various local Thai officials were opposed to the Bond team filming on the island, believing that their presence would be a desecration of the area. But today, it has the nickname 'James Bond island' and is a major tourist attraction in South-east Asia.

But the highlight of *The Man With the Golden Gun* is undoubtedly the lengthy chase sequence. It starts with a race of narrow boats along the narrow canals the Thais call *klongs* and ends up on the road. Bond has hijacked a car in which the passenger is none other than the garrulous red-neck Sheriff J.W. Pepper. As Bond races along, the action is peppered with the sheriff's patronizing comments – 'Go get 'em, boy', 'Press that pedal, boy' – until he is outmanoeuvred by Scaramanga who has managed to switch

to the other side of a canal. There now follows a spectacular stunt (which silences the worthy sheriff once and for all). The car, an American Motors Hornet Hatchback, takes a run at a broken bridge, jumps the gap and does a tremendous 360-degree roll in the process. The jump was programmed by computer at New York's Cornell University Aeronautical Laboratory and the specially adapted car had to hit the ramp at exactly the right speed and angle to achieve the feat. It was the first – and only – time this daring jump had ever been attempted on film.

The stunt worked so perfectly on the first take that Broccoli, relieved at not having to set it up again, gave the driver a $1,000 bonus on the spot. Its successful execution created one of the most extraordinary and memorable stunts seen in a James Bond movie.

DOSSIER

007 THE MAN WITH THE GOLDEN GUN   1974   125 minutes

Producers
Harry Saltzman, Albert R. Broccoli
for Eon Productions

Director
Guy Hamilton

Scriptwriters
Richard Maibaum, Tom Mankiewicz

Directors of photography
Ted Moore, Oswald Morris

Production designer
Peter Murton

Special effects
John Stears

Astro spiral car jump
W. Jay Milligan

Editors
John Shirley, Raymond Poulton

Main title designer
Maurice Binder

Music
composed, conducted and arranged
by John Barry

Title song
lyrics by Don Black, sung by Lulu

Distributor
United Artists

Cast includes
Roger Moore (James Bond)
Christopher Lee (Scaramanga)
Britt Ekland (Mary Goodnight)
Maud Adams (Andrea)
Hervé Villechaize (Nick Nack)
Clifton James (Sheriff J. W. Pepper)
Bernard Lee (M)
Soon-Taik Oh (Hip)
Lois Maxwell (Miss Moneypenny)
Desmond Llewelyn (Q)

Locations
filmed on location in Hong Kong,
Macao, Thailand
and at Pinewood Studios, England

THE SPY WHO LOVED ME

Roger Moore firmly established himself as the Bond of the Seventies in this encounter with a female Soviet spy who comes close to outclassing 007 at the espionage game.

After *The Man With the Golden Gun*, the long-running association between Broccoli and Saltzman as the joint producers of the James Bond series came to an end when Saltzman left the partnership to carry on producing elsewhere. In addition, the next Bond film, *The Spy Who Loved Me*, had had unusual conditions placed on it by Fleming who had allowed the producers to use the title but not the storyline of his book of the same name. So without a novel to act even as a starting point for the film, the Bond team were free to come up with a totally fresh set of ideas.

They decided to tackle head-on one of the long-running criticisms of the Bond series – its sexism – and introduced a female spy, as capable and accomplished in her field as Bond himself. Major Anya Amasova, Soviet agent XXX, is one of the most interesting Bond girls to date, a complete professional counterpart to 007. Her presence provides plenty of opportunity for humour and romance as well as numerous tongue-in-cheek digs at Bond's own chauvinism. Major Anya Amasova is given a rare chance to even things up on that score.

The pre-title sequence sets the scene nicely. Two nuclear submarines – one British, one Soviet – mysteriously disappear and agents 007 and XXX are sent for by their respective secret services. The scene then changes to a bedroom where a Russian couple are making love. The telephone rings. It is General Gogol (the Soviet equivalent of M) wishing to speak to agent XXX. But, in a neat reversal of the audience's expectations, it is not the man but the woman who answers the call.

At the same time, 007 is also predictably entwined in an amorous interlude. His lover, however, proves treacherous, and he has to flee from a gang of Soviet agents. The ski chase that follows (reminiscent of the one in *On Her Majesty's Secret Service* and filmed by the same team, director John Glen and cameraman Willy Bogner) is notable for the most daring Bond stunt to date. With his pursuers hard on his heels, 007 nonchalantly skis over the edge of a massive precipice. As he falls into the depths below, there seems to be no hope for James Bond. Then suddenly he sprouts a parachute, ironically made from a Union Jack, and he lands safely down on the ground.

The stunt was performed by ace skier Rick Sylvester who had never performed such a stunt before. The Asgard, a 1000 m (3000 ft) sheer drop in a Canadian National Park on Baffin Island, proved to be the perfect location for the stunt and several camera crews waited for ideal conditions in order to capture the jump on film. The result is a truly death-defying feat – an ideal opening to a Bond movie. Indeed, at the world *première* of *The Spy Who Loved Me* at London's Leicester Square Odeon (where the majority of the films of the Bond series have had their first showing), the audience broke into spontaneous applause, cheering the audacity of this sequence.

The Assignment

The nuclear submarines have disappeared without trace. Their paths should have been top secret but there exists microfilm evidence that someone has been able to track them. It is suspected that some kind of heat-signature-recognition system (equivalent to locating a ship from its wake) is being used and 007 is sent off to recover the microfilm. So is agent XXX.

After initial skirmishes in Cairo, the British and Soviets join forces to find the submarine stealer. They suspect that Stromberg, a marine biologist with his own vast laboratories, is behind the disappearances and they go to his headquarters in Sardinia to investigate. Their suspicions are confirmed and when Stromberg kidnaps a third nuclear submarine, the two agents are on board. They learn that Stromberg intends to program his first two submarines to fire missiles at Moscow and New York, thus beginning the process of global destruction. Stromberg can then create his own dream world in cities beneath the seas.

Equipment Issued

The Spy Who Loved Me is packed with gadgets. Bond has a watch which spews out ticker-tape messages from M, a cigarette box and lighter which combine to form a microfilm reader, a ski stick that fires bullets and a motor-bike which rides on water. Known as a wetbike, this was a very recent invention which was marketed commercially after the film's release.

Left *It may look as if Bond is up to his usual tricks. In fact, his advances are designed to steal the cassette that Major Anya Amasova (Barbara Bach) has concealed about her person.*

Left *James Bond rides out to Stromberg's Atlantis complex on his latest gadget, a high-speed sea scooter known as a wet bike.*

Bottom *This production shot shows that the ocean is no barrier for Bond's Lotus Esprit. Esprits are hand-made; as a result only five or six are produced each week. This model was converted for its underwater work by the Florida-based Perry Oceanographics Company.*

Below *Underwater driving does, however, have its own particular hazards, as Bond reveals on resurfacing.*

Right *Stromberg's underwater base rises up to the surface. The underwater sequences were shot in the Bahamas.*

The *pièce de résistance* of this film is a new car, replacing the famous Aston Martin last seen in *On Her Majesty's Secret Service*. Bond has a white Lotus Esprit which, in addition to the usual amazing array of armaments, has the ability to travel underwater to a depth of 13 m (42 ft). The car, designed by the Bond team in collaboration with Lotus engineers, is seen at its best in a lengthy chase sequence which begins when Bond and Amasova, posing as a marine biologist and his wife, leave Stromberg's headquarters. They are travelling along a high mountain road when they are met by their first assailant who is on a Kawasaki 900 motor-bike with side-car. It launches a rocket attack on the Lotus Esprit. With some fancy driving, Bond manoeuvres it into a truck containing feather mattresses. Next, a Ford Taunus appears on the scene. Bond forces it over the edge of the cliff by spraying paint onto its windscreen. (The paint ejectors are located behind the Lotus' rear number plates.) Finally, a helicopter moves into the attack. Bond drives over the edge of a jetty and straight into the sea – his passenger is not surprised, however, since she stole the plans for the car two years ago. As the car sinks, it transforms into a two-person submarine and Bond escapes once again. It surfaces on to a crowded beach in Sardinia to looks of utter amazement from the holiday bathers.

By now in the Bond series, it has become an amusing formula to see Q and his assistants testing out new apparatus. In *The Spy Who Loved Me* this scene occurs inside a pyramid where M and General Gogol have set up a joint war-room. Q's Egyptian branch are perfecting gadgets that eject knives or people, an opium pipe which doubles as a gun and a tray which floats across a table decapitating guests at a tea-party. These scenes have become a neat way of mixing technology and visual humour.

Enemy Personnel

Karl Stromberg

Stromberg is a Bond villain in the Blofeld mould. He is a wealthy, powerful man whose personal obsession constitutes a major threat to world civilization. Unlike Blofeld, however, he is not interested in extortion but is fanatically dedicated to the underwater world. For Stromberg, society is doomed because it has embarked on the process of decadent decline and only the dawn of a new sub-aquatic civilization can save it.

His base, a startlingly futuristic creation known as Atlantis, is a vast, black, radial construction which is a prototype for an underwater city. It can survive completely submerged or it can rise up out of the water like a huge metallic spider.

Like Blofeld before him, Stromberg has his own particularly nasty way of dealing with disloyal subordinates – his personal lift turns into a chute which deposits the offending person into a handy shark pool. Through screens in his opulent dining room, Stromberg can then observe their demise in all its gory detail from the comfort of his armchair. Curt Jurgens, who had been in films since he was a teenager but came to international attention playing Germans in Hollywood war movies, is a particularly convincing villain. He is capable of combining menace with a cultured veneer, making his fantastic intentions seem almost within the bounds of possibility.

In his final showdown with Bond on Atlantis, Stromberg uses a hidden gun with its long barrel running the length of his full-size dining table. But 007 moves out of the way in time and returns his fire by using the same gun barrel in reverse – which neatly hoists Stromberg with his own petard.

When this scene was being filmed, the charge went off seconds before it was supposed to, nearly wounding Moore in the process. He is, in fact, quoted as saying that this was the nearest he came to serious injury while working on the Bond films.

Below *Stromberg (Curt Jurgens), resplendent at his dining table, meets his untimely end when Bond returns his fire with the gun that Stromberg had hidden under the table.*

Bottom *Stromberg confronts Major Amasova in his underwater laboratory. Note in particular the windows through which Stromberg can watch all the weird and wonderful creatures of the ocean deep.*

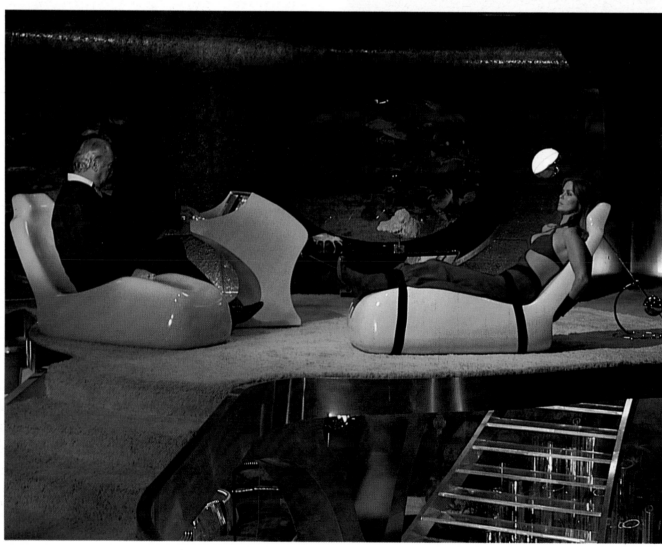

Jaws

Stromberg's minder, the indestructible Jaws, is undoubtedly the best Bond henchman since Oddjob in *Goldfinger*. His metal teeth can bite their way through anything from chains to people. In fact his favourite method of disposal is to sever his victim's jugular vein with his lethal molars. A gigantic tank of a man, Jaws can survive any attack from traditional punches to car crashes, or from less orthodox hazards including falling masonry and being pushed off trains. The train fight echoes equivalent train scenes in *From Russia With Love* and *Live and Let Die*; but at its climax Bond tries to

electrocute Jaws with a broken light switch (succeeding only in throwing him out of the window). He is played by 2.3 m (7 ft 4 in) tall Richard Kiel who endows Jaws with a silent charm, making him quite a sympathetic character.

In Atlantis, towards the end of the film, Bond and Jaws embark on their final encounter. Despite the giant's unbeatable strength, Bond manages to best him by attracting him (literally) to a magnet which picks Jaws up by the teeth and drops him into Stromberg's shark pool. But while Atlantis blows up, Jaws is busy eating the sharks and he lives to fight another day or, to be more precise, in another film . . . *Moonraker*.

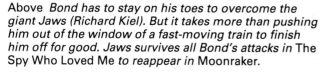

Above *Bond has to stay on his toes to overcome the giant Jaws (Richard Kiel). But it takes more than pushing him out of the window of a fast-moving train to finish him off for good. Jaws survives all Bond's attacks in* The Spy Who Loved Me *to reappear in* Moonraker.

Right *Even a shark is no match for the steel-toothed Jaws – he is quite capable of making a meal out of it.*

The Bond Girl

Major Anya Amasova

This Bond girl is a new phenomenon. Played by Barbara Bach (whose husband is Ringo Starr) she is a top Soviet agent, as revered for her professional triumphs in her own country as Bond is in his. There is, therefore, a certain amount of rivalry between the two of them, even when they are working on the same side. The competition is sharpened (and made funnier) by Bond's inability to accept that a woman can be competent at her job. After all, we all know what 007 thinks women are good for! But Amasova continually turns up trumps, competing with Bond in knowledge, in tactics and even in chases, despite, on one occasion, being inappropriately dressed in evening gown and high-heeled shoes.

One of her best scenes occurs when she and Bond have followed Jaws to an Egyptian ruin. In the fight that follows, Bond survives only by causing a pillar to collapse, imprisoning Jaws in a tumble of falling bricks and mortar. Jaws picks himself up from the wreckage to chase the pair who are trying to escape in the van which Amasova is driving. While Bond keeps up a patronizing monologue ('Try reverse – that's backwards') and Jaws rips off the roof of the car and methodically tries to demolish the rest, Amasova keeps her cool. Finally outmanoeuvring Jaws, she turns to Bond, commenting wryly, 'Shaken, but not stirred'.

There is added spice to the relationship between Bond and Amasova. It becomes clear that in the pre-title sequence Bond killed her lover with his shooting ski-stick and, despite their close relationship on the job, she is determined to kill her British counterpart when the mission is over. So when they are finally settled on the comfy white cushions of Stromberg's escape capsule, fleeing the explosions on Atlantis, Amasova gets out her gun. But instead of taking her revenge, she relents (even Soviet agents eventually fall for Bond's charm it seems) and uses her weapon to uncork a celebratory bottle of champagne.

The Victim

Naomi

Stromberg's beautiful assistant is played by ex-photographic model Caroline Munro. Her part is rather short-lived. Apart from showing Bond and Amasova around Atlantis (giving Barbara Bach plenty of opportunity to practice her smouldering looks as Bond eyes up Naomi) she also turns out to be the helicopter pilot who is trying to kill Bond. She cheerfully carries on a flirtation while shooting at him but ends up the victim of a rocket launched from the underwater Lotus Esprit.

The Background Story

The *tour de force* of *The Spy Who Loved Me* is the *Liparus*, Stromberg's supertanker, which is capable of opening up its bow and swallowing submarines

wholesale. The inside of the tanker can hold three nuclear submarines as well as a characteristic display of elevators, walkways, monorails and an operations room. The biggest stage in the world was built at Pinewood Studios to house the supertanker. Dubbed the '007 stage', it was 102 m (336 ft) long with an extra 12 m (38 ft) tank on the end, 49 m (160 ft) wide and 16 m (53 ft) high. Owned by United Artists and Eon Productions, it cost £350,000 (over $600,000 at the time) and paid for itself through hirings to other productions, before it was burnt down prior to the making of *A View to a Kill*. The rebuilt stage shows no signs of the disaster.

Once again, the climactic fight inside the *Liparus* is spectacular with the red-costumed Stromberg technicians fending off the black-uniformed submarine crews.

Having secured the ground, the allied forces have to break into the control room and Bond steals the detonator from an atomic bomb to force an entry. With only four minutes to go before the nuclear destruction of Moscow and New York, Bond manages to reprogram the submarines to destroy each other, a neat finesse to Stromberg's wily plot.

Below left *Three captured submarines fill the interior of the world's largest film stage, especially built for* The Spy Who Loved Me. *It took seven months to construct the set which is the inside of the 600,000-ton super-tanker* Liparus.

Right *A tense moment as Bond removes the detonator from one of Stromberg's captured atomic bombs. If the detonator touches the inner ring of the bomb, it will blow up taking Bond and the crew of the US submarine with it.*

DOSSIER

007 THE SPY WHO LOVED ME   1977   125 minutes

Producer Albert R. Broccoli for Eon Productions	*Action arranger* Bob Simmons	*Distributor* United Artists
Director Lewis Gilbert	*Ski jump* Rick Sylvester	*Cast includes* Roger Moore (James Bond) Barbara Bach (Major Anya Amasova)
Scriptwriters Christopher Wood, Richard Maibaum	*Editor* John Glen	Curt Jurgens (Karl Stromberg) Richard Kiel (Jaws)
Director of photography Claude Renoir	*Main title designer* Maurice Binder	Caroline Munro (Naomi) Bernard Lee (M) Geoffrey Keen (Minister of Defence)
Production designer Ken Adam (Academy Award nomination)	*Music* by Marvin Hamlisch (Academy Award nomination)	George Baker (Captain Benson) Lois Maxwell (Miss Moneypenny) Desmond Llewelyn (Q)
Cameramen: ski; underwater Willy Bogner; Lamar Boren	*Song* 'Nobody Does It Better' lyrics by Carole Bayer Sager,	*Locations* filmed on location in Egypt,
Special effects Derek Meddings, Alan Maley	sung by Carly Simon (Academy Award nomination)	Sardinia, Bahamas, Canada, Malta, Scotland, Okinawa, Switzerland
2nd Unit directors Ernest Day, John Glen		and at Pinewood Studios, England

MOONRAKER

*007 enters the space age in this adventure which became the all-time
record-breaking Bond movie.*

At the end of *The Spy Who Loved Me, For Your Eyes
Only* was announced as the next Bond adventure.
But with the American space shuttle in the news,
the Bond team decided to make *Moonraker* first, it
being the only Fleming title left with a space theme.
With films like *Star Wars* and *Close Encounters of the
Third Kind* packing the crowds into cinemas, *Moonraker* had a lot to live up to. But with all the usual
Bond elements present, many of which are given a
new twist when located in outer space, it proved to
be the biggest financial success of the Bond films to
date.

The die-hard Fleming buffs, however, were disappointed with *Moonraker*, but the younger Bond
fans who had grown up with the movies rather than
the books gave it an enthusiastic reception. *Moonraker* was moving with the times and, like many films
of the period, it includes in-joke references to other
films. This trend, which started with *The Spy Who
Loved Me* (the theme music from *Lawrence of Arabia* is
heard when Bond and Amasova are crossing the
desert on foot), was continued in *Moonraker* with
spoofs on *Close Encounters of the Third Kind* (the
coded bell-push to a secret laboratory plays the
immediately recognizable four-note call sign from
that film) and *The Magnificent Seven* (its theme music
is heard when Bond is riding across Brazil wearing a
poncho). These newer aspects of Bond traditions
undoubtedly helped the film's popularity with
younger audiences who revel in this kind of
humour.

The pre-title sequence, conceived by executive
producer Michael G. Wilson, includes another
seemingly impossible escape. After the space theme
has been introduced, the scene changes to the
interior of an airplane where Bond is engaged in his
usual amorous activities with an air hostess. She
turns out to be an enemy agent and smashes the
plane controls; when she and the pilot are
preparing to parachute off the plane leaving Bond
stranded, a fight begins. Bond pushes the pilot out
of the plane and he, in turn, is pushed out –
parachuteless – behind him.

In the astounding stunt that follows, Bond sky-
dives down like a bullet to catch up with the pilot,
wrestles his parachute off him and puts it on
himself. But just when he thought it was safe to get
back to earth, Jaws (the massive villain from *The Spy
Who Loved Me*) follows behind him and tries the
same trick. Bond escapes by opening his parachute
to slow his rate of descent at just the right moment,
leaving Jaws to crash down into a circus big top
below, conveniently landing in the safety net.

The Assignment

The Moonraker space shuttle, transported from
the US to Britain on the back of a Boeing 747, has
been hijacked in mid-air and the Jumbo destroyed.
The shuttle is the latest in rocket technology – it can
be launched into space and orbit the earth but can
then re-enter earth's atmosphere and land like a
conventional aircraft. As the shuttle was on loan
from the Americans, the matter is serious and Bond
is sent off to discover who stole the shuttle and why.

Drax Industries, in the Mojave Desert in California, is where the shuttle was built and this is
Bond's starting point. His enquiries there produce
serious misgivings about Mr Drax himself, suspicions which lead him to Venice. Here he learns
that Drax has developed a deadly nerve gas which

Above *In the pre-title sequence, Bond battles with the
pilot of the plane who is trying to push him out without a
parachute.*

Left *Drax's space station – the most menacing satellite to
revolve around the earth.*

kills people but not other wildlife. The gas comes from a rare orchid found in remote regions of Brazil – which is his next stop. He finally locates Drax's secret headquarters only to find that Drax is up to something supremely sinister. He has built a city in space which he intends to populate with beautiful people (flown there by the Moonraker shuttles) who will become the progenitors of a new super-race. At the same time, he intends to kill off earth's population with the nerve gas, leaving the super-race to construct a new, ordered civilization on earth in the future.

Left *As his speedboat approaches the gushing torrents of the Iguacu Falls which mark the boundary between Brazil and Argentina, James Bond soars away from danger with his detachable hang-glider.*

Below *Christened 'the Bondola' by the film crew, 007's unique craft makes a dramatic entry into St Mark's Square in Venice by turning from a gondola into a motor launch and then into a hovercraft.*

Right *Drax (Michael Lonsdale), who plans to establish a colony of supermen and women in his space city, takes the controls of his command station.*

Equipment Issued

Q presents Bond with the new standard-issue watch for British Secret Service agents. Apart from telling the time, it can also shoot out darts (either armour-piercing or poisoned) by means of a flick of the wrist. It is an exceedingly useful gadget which saves Bond several times in the adventures to come. He also has a collection of other ingenious devices: a safe-cracking gadget which operates by means of X-rays; a mini-camera, the lens of which is in the 0 of the 007 printed on it; and a streamlined boat for crossing the Brazilian jungle waterways. The boat is used to evade 007's pursuers and, as Bond approaches a giant waterfall, he presses a switch and the top of the boat pulls off, turning into a hang-glider which lands him safely on the river bank below.

As always, Q's gadgets are specially designed for their country of operation. In Brazil, his assistants are there in force testing out a variety of gimmicks (in a rich display of visual humour), and in Venice he gives Bond a unique gondola. When Bond is attacked by a man hidden in a passing coffin, the gondola becomes a motor-launch. He is chased through the canals of Venice but finally escapes at St Mark's Square (where the astute viewer can spot producer Broccoli walking across the piazza) when the motor-launch becomes a hovercraft – to the bemusement of the tourists.

Enemy Personnel

Hugo Drax

The head of Drax Industries, Mr Hugo Drax is another of Bond's rather refined opponents. It is Drax who has single-handedly financed the American space-shuttle programme, building the *Moonraker* and training the astronauts – albeit for his own devious ends. He appears to be a veritable pillar of the establishment and is even on drinking terms with the British Minister of Defence. He lives in an elegant French château (brought to California from France brick by brick) which is complete with antique furniture and old masters. He clearly enjoys the good things of life – like pheasant shooting, where he tries to arrange Bond's 'accidental' death – and entertains a particular disgust for the degeneration of contemporary society, preferring his dream of a new world among the stars.

The location for Drax's château was found at the magnificent Vaux-le-Vicomte which is like a mini-Versailles some 80 km (50 miles) outside Paris. The château was built in the seventeenth century by Louis XIV's minister of finance who hosted a lavish feast on its completion. Louis XIV, so the story goes, took one look at the magnificent surroundings and furnishings and promptly threw his minister in jail for embezzlement.

Played by Michael Lonsdale, perhaps best remembered as the French detective who foils the assassin in Fred Zinnemann's *The Day of the Jackal*, Drax is a very cultured villain. He is in his element addressing the beautiful people aboard his city in the sky with all the demonic fervour of the obsessed. He meets an appropriate end. Having been speared with a poisoned dart from 007's watch, he is pushed out through an airlock by Bond who thus despatches his adversary to enjoy the vast, empty regions of outer space until he dies.

Chang

Drax's first henchman is Chang, played by black-belt judo expert Toshiro Suga. He has two attempts at disposing of Bond. His first occurs when Bond is trying out the centrifugal machine which prepares astronauts to cope with G-forces. Echoing Count Lippe's use of the 'rack' in *Thunderball*, Chang speeds up the machine beyond the limit of human endurance until Bond smashes the controls with a dart from his watch, released with a flick of his wrist.

Chang tries again in Venice where, dressed in traditional Japanese fighting gear, he attacks Bond in Drax's museum of antique glass. Unfortunately, it is most of the priceless glass exhibits that fall victim to Chang's stave rather than 007 who is fighting back with a rare glass-handled sword. Chang meets his demise at the end of the fight when Bond pushes him through a magnificent glass clock.

Above Bond has a smashing time with Chang (Toshiro Suga) behind the face of the Venetian 15th-century Merceria clock which indicates the passing of the seasons. It is also the setting for the passing of Chang.

Below Jaws (Richard Kiel) has finally met his match – his tiny sweetheart, Dolly. She is played by Blanche Ravalec, a French actress (who was formerly an airline stewardess).

Jaws

With Chang out of the picture, Drax needs another protector and who should he call for but the indestructible Jaws. He tries to kill Bond by pushing him off a cable-car lift *en route* to one of Rio's heights. The duel that follows is fought out on top of two cable cars suspended high above the ground. It is a nail-biting scene but Bond finally manages to slide down the cable to safety leaving Jaws to crash into the terminal below. Predictably, Jaws survives – and meets a soulmate in the rubble, a diminuitive buck-toothed miss with hair in plaits called Dolly.

This unlikely romance turns out to be a life-saver for Bond. When trapped by Drax in the space city, he points out to Jaws that Drax's plans involve only physically perfect human specimens. Jaws slowly works out that this does not apply either to him or to his new-found love and promptly changes sides. Jaws, who has always been a popular villain, becomes a goodie; and after helping Bond to escape, he and Dolly are picked up by a US spacecraft as survivors of the space city.

The Bond Girl

Dr Holly Goodhead

Bond, who still retains his chauvinism even after his encounter with Major Amasova in *The Spy Who Loved Me*, is amazed to find that one of Drax's space consultants, Dr Holly Goodhead, is a woman. She is a fully-trained astronaut on loan from NASA to Drax Industries who also turns up in Venice, osten-

sibly to address a seminar at the European Space Commission. She also happens to be a CIA agent.

Forming a partnership with the Americans proves to be more difficult than with the Soviets in the previous film, but Bond never gives up where a woman is concerned. When the pair do finally combine resources, they head off into outer space in one of the Moonraker shuttles to do battle with Drax.

Bond identifies Dr Goodhead as an agent by her standard CIA issue devices – a set of gadgets which

Above *Dr Holly Goodhead (Lois Chiles) is another extremely capable Bondian heroine. Apart from being an expert astrophysicist and an astronaut – she is also a CIA agent.*

Left *A well-placed kick to a member of Drax's space crew clearly demonstrates Dr Goodhead's expertise in unarmed combat.*

rival Q's ingenuity. She has a pen with a poisoned point (which proves extremely useful when Bond later faces an encounter with an amorous anaconda), an address book which fires darts, a perfume spray which sets things alight and a good line in punches. She is another 007 counterpart who has difficulty proving her capabilities to a sceptical Bond.

When they find themselves in the space shuttle, however, Dr Goodhead with her superior astronautical knowledge and training is clearly in control. Her familiarity with space procedures and technology proves invaluable at every turn. Lois Chiles, who previously made a career of appearing as victims in films such as *Coma* and *Death on the Nile*, makes a very credible agent, equally at home in the laboratory or in the field. As Goodhead and Bond speed away from the destruction of Drax's space city in the *Moonraker*, she notches one up on previous Bond girls when she gets her sexual thrills with 007 in the weightless atmosphere of outer space.

The Victim

Corinne Dufour

Another Bond-film victim who enters the scenario only to leave it a few scenes later is Corinne Dufour. She is played by Corinne Clery, discovered by film director Just Jaekin who cast her in his *The Story of 'O'*. Miss Dufour is Bond's guide around Drax Industries. Unluckily for her, Bond's ardour sweeps her away and she ends up revealing the location of Drax's safe. Her reward is not only instant dismissal but also to be hounded to death by Drax's large, black hunting dogs.

The Background Story

Broccoli argued that *Moonraker* was not science fiction, like other contemporary movies, but science fact and great efforts were taken in the planning of the film to ensure authenticity. Ken Adam's flights of fantasy are limited to Drax's launching station housed inside an ancient Brazilian temple. Lush vegetation and water are combined on the outside with ancient monuments and modern metallic walkways. But inside all is high-tech, and when the shuttles depart for the space city, the sets become even more futuristic while being anchored in what scientists believe will one day be reality.

Special-effects man Derek Meddings spent some time extensively researching space technology, and two consultants from NASA were hired for the film. As a tribute to NASA's help with the film, the *première* of *Moonraker* was to have been in Houston (the home of NASA's Mission Control Center), within a week of the first space-shuttle flight. But technical problems with the shuttle delayed the launch and the film had its *première* as usual, in London at the Odeon, Leicester Square.

The worthwhile result of this research and advice is a gigantic space station, built on three tiers at France's Epinay Studios, whose massive banks of computers, and video monitors make it look realistic rather than fantastic. The space station contains the largest amount of material ever used to build a film set, with Adam's tubular designs providing an ideal backdrop for the technological hardware.

The final battle, fought in space between the would-be colonists and the US astronaut army, involved a medley of visual and optical effects, many of which had been developed especially for

Left *Not the kind of embrace that 007 is used to! Bond wrestles with a giant anaconda in the pool of Drax's subterranean launch site in Brazil.*

Above right *The crew members of Drax's space station experience the problems of weightlessness. This gigantic set resembles a giant molecular structure with huge spheres connected by tubes and banks of solar reflectors. Built on three tiers, it took 220 technicians some 8 weeks to contruct at France's Epinay Studios.*

this film. Real people and real lasers had to be integrated with models and simulated lasers; the combatants had to appear weightless; the stage had to be shrouded in black velvet to prevent light being scattered; and efforts were made to make the stars look like real pinpoints of steady light rather than speckled walls. The explosions in space for the battle had to look believable, an extremely difficult task given that, unlike earthly explosions, they cannot emit either smoke or flames in the airless atmosphere of outer space. In addition, model shots, live action on full-scale sets, location shooting, front and back projection with models and front and back projection with live actresses – all this had to be combined to film one scene.

The result was a highly unusual Bond-movie climax and one undoubtedly in tune with the mood of the times.

DOSSIER

007 MOONRAKER 1979 126 minutes

Producer
Albert R. Broccoli
for Les Productions Artistes Associés
(United Artists) and Eon Productions

Executive producer
Michael G. Wilson

Director
Lewis Gilbert

Scriptwriter
Christopher Wood

Director of photography
Jean Tournier

Production designer
Ken Adam

Action unit directors
Ernest Day, John Glen

Visual special effects
Derek Meddings
(Academy Award nomination)

Stunt arranger
Bob Simmons

Editor
John Glen

Main title designer
Maurice Binder

Music
by John Barry

Title song
lyrics by Hal David,
sung by Shirley Bassey

Distributor
United Artists

Cast includes
Roger Moore (James Bond)
Lois Chiles (Holly Goodhead)
Michael Lonsdale (Drax)
Richard Kiel (Jaws)
Corinne Clery (Corinne Dufour)
Bernard Lee (M)
Emily Bolton (Manuela)
Toshiro Suga (Chang)
Irka Bochenko (blonde beauty)
Geoffrey Keen (Minister of Defence)
Lois Maxwell (Miss Moneypenny)
Desmond Llewelyn (Q)
Walter Gotell (General Gogol)

Locations
filmed on location in Italy, Brazil,
Guatemala, USA and at Boulogne,
Eclair and Paris Studios, France
and Pinewood Studios, England

FOR YOUR EYES ONLY

*The Bond movies return to their earlier taut style with this pacy thriller
set among the Greek underworld.*

For Your Eyes Only, closely based on two short stories by Fleming in the collection of the same title, breaks all the rules of the Bond film formulae. There is no supervillain bent on destroying civilization, no race against time to save the world from some dastardly threat and no climactic explosion of the villain's headquarters. What there is in *For Your Eyes Only* is a taut thriller based in the complex milieu of the Greek underworld where it is never quite clear exactly who is on whose side. The new Bond director John Glen returns to the feel of the first Bond movies to some extent. Yet despite the change in the plot construction, many of the later traditions remain.

The titles, designed as usual by Maurice Binder, are innovatory in that they show, for the first time in any movie, the singer of the title song. Sheena Easton, who performs the song, is a typical Bond choice – and the song of 'For Your Eyes Only' won an Academy Award.

The pre-title sequence is a joke in itself. After visiting the grave of his dead wife – a rare reference to Tracy (from *On Her Majesty's Secret Service*) in a Roger Moore film – 007 is picked up by a Universal Exports helicopter to take him to an important meeting (Universal Exports being the 'front' for the Secret Service). But in mid-flight the pilot is suddenly killed and the controls taken over to remote by a bald man in a wheelchair on a rooftop who is stroking a rather familiar white cat. Could this be Blofeld, one more time, out for revenge?

With the newcomer in charge, the helicopter finds itself performing some daring stunts, nearly grazing buildings, just missing bridges and flying straight into a deserted warehouse. Clearly whatever the identity of the bald man, he is relishing Bond's discomfort to the full before giving him the *coup de grâce*. But, of course, Bond finds a way out. He climbs out of the helicopter and into the pilot's seat, disconnects the remote control lead, scoops up the unnamed man, wheelchair and all, on the helicopter skids and drops his unwilling passenger down a nearby chimney stack. With the joking out of the way, the serious action can begin.

The Assignment

The *St Georges*, a British electronic surveillance ship disguised as a fishing boat, has been blown up in the Ionian Sea. On board is the valuable ATAC

machine, an Automatic Targeting Attack Communicator which is a coded transmitter using ultra-low frequencies to order British submarines to launch their ballistic missiles. In the wrong hands, the entire Polaris fleet could be rendered useless – or worse, the submarines could be instructed to attack British cities with no chance of the order being manually countermanded. Salvage operations have begun and among the interested parties is General Gogol of the Soviet Secret Service. Bond is sent off to locate the ATAC transmitter and stop the enemy getting hold of it.

Above *Bond circles his helicopter over an industrial smokestack in London before making a drop that will dispose of some unwanted human refuse in this scene from the pre-title sequence.*

Left *Carole Bouquet plays Melina. Her expertise with a crossbow proves most helpful to 007 throughout the film.*

He has one lead: marine archeologist Sir Timothy Havelock was murdered while searching for the ATAC on behalf of the British. His killer, a well-known Cuban hit-man named Gonzales, lives in Madrid. Bond pays his villa a visit but before he can learn who killed Havelock, Gonzales is himself killed by a bolt from a crossbow and Bond's lead dries up. However, before Gonzales died Bond did see him being paid for his 'hit' by a man wearing octagonal silver-framed glasses. If he can identify the man, he might still have a clue to work from.

Equipment Issued

Apart from a red Lotus Esprit (replacing the white one which self-destructs in Madrid when somebody tries to break one of its windows), Bond has little equipment to help him in his task, for this is not a traditionally gadget-packed Bond movie.

Q nevertheless provides considerable assistance in identifying the man who paid off Gonzales. He does this by means of his new toy, a 3-D visual identigraph which first composes an identikit picture of the suspect from information fed into it and then taps into the photographic files of all the Western police agencies – the Sureté, Interpol and the CIA to name but a few – to find a match. It is the excuse for a nice scene in which Q, who is clearly getting too old for these new-fangled machines, plays at the controls trying to make a picture from Bond's instructions.

Above *Bond is skating on thin ice when he is cornered in a deserted hockey rink in Cortina. But he manages to keep his footing and defeat his would-be assassin.*

Below *Bond comes to the rescue to save Melina on the snowy streets of Cortina. In fact, when the crew arrived in the famous winter resort there was no snow on the streets and so truckloads had to be brought in each morning from the surrounding mountains.*

Enemy Personnel

Emile Locque

The man identified by Q's identigraph is Emile Locque, an impassive, ruthless killer whose octagonal silver-framed glasses distinguish him from other hoods. He is known to be working for a powerful Greek smuggler but Bond's problem is who? So 007 sets off for Cortina d'Ampezzo, a winter ski resort with Olympic facilities, to find Locque.

But it is Locque, aided by two leather-jacketed hit-men on motorbikes and the East German skiing champion, Kriegler, who finds Bond. The gang try to kill him, chasing him across the ski slopes, attacking him in a murderous game of ice hockey, shooting at him on the bob-sleigh run and ganging up against him on the ski jump. The most exciting of these stunts (shot, once again, by Willy Bogner) is on the bob-sleigh run where a motorbike chases Bond on skis who is himself skiing behind a sleigher round the twists and turns of the run. Bond asserts his excellence at all forms of winter sports to evade the gang's murderous intentions.

Locque, played by Michael Gothard who has made a TV career out of playing psychopaths, killers and rapists, is a dedicated professional. With his band of assistants, he makes a second attack on Bond in Corfu, both on the beach and again in a smuggler's warehouse. After a lengthy fight, Locque tries to run Bond down by car but ends up with his vehicle straddled over a sheer drop. With the helpful kick from Bond, he and his car crash down onto the rocks below.

Columbo and Kristatos

Bond's problem is to identify Locque's master. It could be either Columbo, a jovial rogue who is involved in all kinds of petty crime, or Kristatos, a Greek magnate whose occupation is supplying information to interested parties. During the war, both men fought together as partisans but later each claimed the other had turned traitor and now both are out for revenge. Kristatos tells Bond that Locque is working for Columbo, known ironically, he explains, as the Dove. Columbo, when Bond finally gets to meet him, argues that it is Kristatos who is really the paymaster.

Kristatos is played by Julian Glover, a well-known British stage actor who has also made his mark in a variety of film and TV roles, while Columbo is played by Topol, the endearing Israeli actor who made his name in the West with the stage and screen versions of *Fiddler on the Roof*.

Kristatos has a young protégée – a precocious teenage ice-skater with Olympic ambitions. Bibi, played by Lynn-Holly Johnson, a child actress turned professional skater, also has ambitions in Bond's direction. But for once, the British Secret Service's most amorous agent turns the invitation down – she is too young. He offers to buy her an ice-cream instead.

Kristatos is cultured and kindly, Columbo is bluff and likeable, but after several skirmishes all becomes clear. It is Kristatos who is working freelance for General Gogol and trying to get hold of the ATAC. Columbo (who gains Bond's trust by returning his Walther PPK to him) helps Bond penetrate Kristatos' cliff-top sanctuary. While Bibi is trying to escape from Kristatos, Bond with the aid of Columbo's men attacks his base. Columbo kills Kristatos and Bibi finds herself a new sponsor.

Carrying the top-secret ATAC stolen from the British Secret Service, Kristatos (Julian Glover) tries to slip away from the scene of a fight in his mountaintop hideout. Fortunately, Bond and Melina are on hand to prevent him getting any further.

Left *Jacoba Brink (Jill Bennett) and Bibi (Lynn-Holly Johnson) tend to the injured Columbo (Topol) after his fight with Kristatos.*

Below *James Bond and Melina are ready to undergo a nasty version of keelhauling devised by Kristatos and face the dangers of sharks and coral reefs beneath the waters.*

The Bond Girl

Melina

Sir Timothy Havelock's daughter Melina was present when her father (and mother) were gunned to death on their yacht and she is determined to avenge them. Being half Greek and half English, she argues that revenge is in her heritage. Melina is played by Carole Bouquet, a French actress who won critical acclaim for her role in Luis Buñuel's *That Obscure Object of Desire*. Inevitably her path crosses that of Bond and, like all the later Bond women, she proves to be an invaluable colleague. She is a dab-hand with a crossbow – it was her bolt that killed Gonzales. Melina is, in fact, Greek for honey – a reminder of the first Bond girl in *Dr No*.

Bond and Melina first met escaping from Gonzales' men. The Lotus Esprit has been blown up, leaving them to flee in Melina's car – a tiny Citroen 2CV. This is one of the more amusing Bond car chases, since what the 2CV lacks in horsepower has to be compensated for with fancy driving and nifty brakework. As the 2CV drives down stairs, turns completely over and carries on, rides down the sides of mountains and jumps over cars with ease it proves to be more manoeuvrable than anything Q has yet dreamed up.

Melina, following in her father's footsteps, is a skilled marine archeologist and helps Bond locate the wreckage of the *St Georges* with the undamaged ATAC still sitting inside it. They are attacked and eventually captured by Kristatos who arranges a bizarre death for the pair of them by dragging them underwater across the coral reef – hoping the sharks will finish them off. Bond makes use of an underwater rock to cut the rope tying them together and they escape back to Melina's yacht, the *Triana*. They then join forces with Columbo to attack Kristatos' base.

After their success in thwarting General Gogol's aims, Melina and Bond conclude their adventure restfully aboard the *Triana*. This leads to a high-satire ending in which top British impersonators Janet Brown and John Wells appear as Margaret and Dennis Thatcher. Mrs T, embroiled in her kitchen, stopping her husband pinching titbits, telephones 007 to give him her personal congratulations. But Bond, who has other things on his mind, puts Melina's talking parrot on the call in his place. It is an unusually cheeky ending for a Bond film and one that caused great mirth among cinemagoers around the world.

The Victim

Countess Lisl

Columbo's girlfriend is the elegant Countess Lisl, played by Cassandra Harris (the wife of Pierce Brosnan who years later became one of the contenders to replace Roger Moore in *The Living Daylights*). Lisl, it transpires, is a native of Liverpool.

When Columbo suspects Bond of spying on him, he stages an argument with her and Bond falls into the trap by taking her home. After spending the night together, they are walking on the beach when they are attacked by Locque and his band of hoodlums, who put an end to the Countess. Bond is saved by men in uniforms emblazoned with white doves and he finally gets to meet Columbo – the Dove – himself.

Above *With 007 in the driving seat, even a Citroen 2CV can perform all kinds of wonders as Bond and Melina race away from Gonzales' men.*

Right *The Countess Lisl (from Liverpool) is played by Australian actress Cassandra Harris. In this scene, she faces up to the problems of the morning after the night with Bond when Locque (Michael Gothard) tries to run her down.*

The final action sequence of the film – in which Bond scales the sheer rock protecting Kristatos' base – is equally breathtaking. It was filmed in the 600-year-old monastery at Meteora near the village of Kalambaka in Greece. Eon Productions became the innocent victims of a dispute between the local monks, who felt their privileges were being invaded, and the local people, who recognized the tourist value of a Bond film shooting in their village. The monks did all they could to stop the shoot – including hanging their washing out while filming was in progress – but the crew carried on regardless, managing to avoid the distractions and producing a sequence full of suspense. The climbing team, headed by Rick Sylvester who made the ski jump from the Asgard in *The Spy Who Loved Me*, creates some tense moments when one of Kristatos' henchmen is trying to unpin Bond's climbing brack-

Left *Larger than the traditional diving suit and rather sinister in appearance, the 'JIM' diving suit is named after Jim Jarratt who located the sunken liner* The Lusitania. *This outfit has four observation windows in its headpiece and its huge arms and legs are fitted with murderous-looking manipulators and pincers.*

Below *Climbing turns out to be another of Bond's skills. It is put to good use when he has single-handedly to scale the heights of Kristatos' stronghold.*

Right *While Melina covers with her crossbow Bond tries to reach the ATAC before it gets into the hands of the fallen Kristatos.*

The Background Story

For Your Eyes Only is graced with some spectacular underwater photography particularly when Melina and Bond are trying to recover the ATAC. Production designer Peter Lamont created an unusual underwater set of the archeological site that Melina is working on. It is the ruins of a Greek temple complete with Ionic columns, half-collapsed arches, fragments of statues and a mosaic floor. Melina even has an underwater vacuum cleaner for clearing up the debris covering the ancient floor.

But it is on the search for the ATAC that the underwater highlights occur with an assortment of exotic underwater vehicles. There is the *Neptune*, Melina's two-person submarine, designed by Lamont for the film; a one-person submersible in which the operator lies prone and is able to use arms outside of the craft to which various tools can be attached; and a unique 'JIM' diving suit, equipped with murderous-looking arms and pincers, which in reality is used for salvage operations. All three pieces of equipment have prominent roles to play in the underwater battle with Kristatos which is finally resolved only when Melina and Bond reboard the *Triana*.

ets and leave him dangling on the end of his rope above the steep drop below. In the fight that follows, Bond, Melina and Columbo recover the ATAC just as General Gogol arrives in a helicopter. Bond picks up the precious ATAC and throws it over the edge of the cliff, arguing that neither he nor Gogol can then have it. After all, as he says, 'That's détente, comrade!'

One sad note was struck during the filming of *For* *Your Eyes Only*. Bernard Lee who had played the part of M, the head of the British Secret Service, in all the Bond films fell ill just before the film went into production. In recognition of his contribution to the Bond series, Broccoli refused to replace him in this film, preferring to create a new character, the Chief of Staff. Lee died shortly after the film's release and in the next Bond, *Octopussy*, M was once again present, this time played by Robert Brown.

DOSSIER

Producer
Albert R. Broccoli
for Eon Productions

Executive producer
Michael G. Wilson

Director
John Glen

Scriptwriters
Richard Maibaum, Michael G. Wilson

Director of photography
Alan Hume

Production designer
Peter Lamont

Action unit director
Arthur Wooster

Special effects supervisor
Derek Meddings

Cameramen: underwater; aerial; ski
Al Giddings; James Devis; Willy Bogner

Action sequences arrangers
Bob Simmons, Remy Julienne

Editor
John Grover

Main title designer
Maurice Binder

Music
by Bill Conti

Title song
lyrics by Michael Leeson,
sung by Sheena Easton
(Academy Award nomination)

Distributor
United Artists

Cast includes
Roger Moore (James Bond)
Carole Bouquet (Melina Havelock)
Topol (Columbo)
Lynn-Holly Johnson (Bibi)
Julian Glover (Kristatos)
Cassandra Harris (Countess Lisl)
Jill Bennett (Jacoba Brink)
Michael Gothard (Locque)
Jack Hedley (Havelock)
Walter Gotell (General Gogol)
Lois Maxwell (Miss Moneypenny)
Desmond Llewelyn (Q)

Locations
filmed on location in Greece,
Italy, the Bahamas, England
and at Pinewood Studios, England

OCTOPUSSY

Chasing forged Russian jewels takes Bond to India where he teams up with an unusually acrobatic female army and enjoys all the fun of the circus ring.

Generally the Bond villains have not been identifiable with any particular country (although the occasional reference to Red China suggests its shadowy presence somewhere in the background). In the early Bond films made in the Sixties, when détente prevailed between Western and Eastern Europe, the villain usually belonged to SPECTRE, a freelance organization whose aims were extortion and world domination. Later Bond opponents might have had contact with the KGB at some point in their lives but were usually working for themselves by the time they came to 007's attention. By the Eighties, however, it was no longer possible to leave the Soviet Union out of the picture and General Gogol was introduced in *The Spy Who Loved Me* as the head of the Soviet Secret Service.

Gogol is the exact counterpart of M, in terms of both status and intentions – which are to maintain peace in the world through preserving the status quo. In *The Spy Who Loved Me*, the British and the Soviets joined forces; in *For Your Eyes Only*, Gogol is on the other side – but only to attain an instrument that is no more than part of the espionage game. In *Octopussy*, he is present again, but for the first time there is a Russian who is behind the threat to world peace. Gogol, with the backing of the Soviet presidium, is still trying to maintain détente; but General Orlov (who with Gogol is a member of the war council) is aiming for war in order to win the

Soviets a world-wide victory. Thus, by bringing dissent into the Soviet ranks, the film-makers found the perfect answer to maintaining an element of realistic diplomatic relations. They had a Russian villain at the same time as having a Soviet leadership who was concerned for peace.

Octopussy is actually lightly based on two of Fleming's short stories. One, *The Property of a Lady*, concerns the sale of a Fabergé egg while in the other, *Octopussy*, Bond uncovers the corruption of Major Dexter Smythe who is mentioned briefly in the film as Octopussy's father. Like most of the Bond films by this time, *Octopussy* takes little more from Fleming than a few ideas, some characters and a title.

Keeping up with the times, *Octopussy* is set very much in the Eighties, in a world where nuclear disarmament is a public controversy in both Western and Eastern Europe. Against this unusually realistic political background, all the traditional Bond movie elements are worked out.

Left *Bond holds one of the famous Fabergé eggs – priceless concoctions of precious stones that were each fitted by Carl Fabergé with a jewelled surprise. After Q gets his hands on this one, it has even more of a surprise to offer.*

Below *The Soviet war room – one of Peter Lamont's creations – makes a rare appearance in a Bond film.*

Left *A narrow escape for Bond in his diminutive AcroStar jet as he flies through the closing doors leaving a heat-seeking missile trapped in the hangar behind him.*

Below *The AcroStar jet stops to fuel up at a gas station. The world's smallest jet boasts a top speed of 496 km/h (310 mph) and a ceiling of 9000 m (30,000 ft). It astounded audiences with its versatility and amazing aerial capabilities.*

The pre-title sequence, by now one of the most popular facets of the Bond movies, again has nothing at all to do with the plot. Somewhere in Latin America, Bond is trying to destroy a spyplane but his cover is blown. In the chase that follows, he manages to reach his own miniature plane hidden in a horsebox and flies away in it. The plane, the AcroStar, is only 3.5 m (12 ft) long with a 5 m (17 ft) wing span and there are only two of its kind in the world. The one in the film is owned and flown by Corkey Fornof of Louisiana, USA.

But having become airborne Bond has still not escaped, for the opposition send up a heat-seeking missile which persists in following the tiny jet however many twists, turns and dives it takes. It is the most tricky situation for Bond yet but (of course) he finds a solution. He flies the plane into the enemy hangar, tilting it to fly back out through the rapidly closing doors but leaving the missile trapped inside. With one clever manoeuvre, Bond has not only escaped but also blown up the original target plane. A few minutes later, 007's jet runs out of fuel and he lands at a gas station to fill up! After this gleefully irrelevant opening, the story proper begins.

The Assignment

In recent months several Fabergé eggs have turned up for auction at international markets. These priceless and rare antiques are jewelled eggs made by Carl Fabergé in 1897 for the Russian royal family and nobody is clear who is selling and why. Even more mysteriously, a realistic fake turns up in the dead hands of agent 009 (who was working under-cover as a circus clown) in East Germany. Now, an egg, enamelled in translucent green, enclosed by laurel-leaved gold trellis work and set with blue sapphires and four gold-petalled flowers with diamonds, is on sale at the famous London auction rooms, Sotheby's. M sends Bond off to find out more about them.

The egg is bought at an inflated price by Kamal Khan whom Bond follows to his home in Udaipur in India. Once there, Bond discovers that Kamal is working as part of a highly organized gang of jewel thieves who are orchestrating a major heist from the Kremlin vaults, replacing the originals (including the Fabergé eggs) with clever fakes. The gang, run by the wealthy and glamorous Octopussy, disguises its activities through its work as the Octopussy circus troop and smuggles the treasures out from East to West on its circus train. At the last moment, Kamal had to buy the egg back to prevent the ruse being discovered.

However, General Orlov, the mastermind of the scheme from the Soviet end, wants to use the circus route for his own, more sinister, plans. He aims, with Kamal's help, to smuggle a small atomic bomb into a US Airforce base in West Germany, placing it where the jewels are usually hidden among the trappings of the circus. When the bomb detonates, Orlov reasons, people will consider the explosion an accident. This should strengthen the argument for nuclear disarmament which will leave Western Europe defenceless and Soviet tanks can then roll in. Needless to say, the Soviet authorities and General Gogol are unaware of this plot, so it is up to Bond to save the situation.

Equipment Issued

Q's Indian station is busy perfecting a range of colourful tricks appropriate to an assignment there but he also has a useful personal device for Bond – a fountain pen. Twist the top and a concentrated mixture of nitric and hydrochloric acid is emitted which can eat its way through most metals. Pull the top off and an ultra-sensitive ear-piece is revealed. Q then puts a miniature homing device (which can be monitored by 007's standard-issue watch) and a microphone (which can be listened in to with the fountain pen) inside the Fabergé egg, Bond having managed to swap 009's fake for the real one at Sotheby's. Bond is able to put all his devices to good use when held prisoner in Kamal's palace: the pen dissolves the bars of his room so he can escape; the homer allows him to find the egg when it is stolen from him by Magda (who is working for Kamal); and the microphone enables him to listen to Kamal and Orlov discussing their plans. All in all, a useful little set of gadgets.

Enemy Personnel

Kamal Khan

The villain of the piece, Kamal Khan, is a wealthy exiled Afghan prince who owns his own palace and a chain of casinos. Played by French actor Louis

Jourdan, known for his romantic leads in American films like *Three Coins in the Fountain* and *Gigi*, Kamal has a taste for the good things in life – from jewels to food (he serves Bond a banquet of soufflé and stuffed sheep's head, including the eyes which are considered a delicacy). At first, when bidding for the egg at Sotheby's, he seems a gentlemanly rogue; but when it becomes clear that he cheats at backgammon, it is obvious that he is far more sinister!

Kamal knows that the Kremlin heist is a cover for a more menacing plan and is actually working for General Orlov rather than Octopussy. He shows his truly evil side when he sets the timer on the atomic bomb (due to detonate when the circus comes to perform at the US Airforce base) and leaves civilians and accomplices alike to die.

Magda

Kamal's beautiful accomplice Magda is played by blonde-haired Swedish actress Kristina Wayborn. She seduces Bond (never a difficult task) in order to recover the real egg. She turns out to be one of Octopussy's troop and the ring-master in her circus. Magda is 'girl number one' of the traditional Bond formula, but unlike her less fortunate predecessors, she is still alive at the end of the film.

Gobinda

Kamal's henchman is the traditionally silent Gobinda, played by Anglo-Indian actor Kabir Bedi who was a matinée idol in Indian films before he moved to America. Gobinda has several attempts at killing Bond: the first after Bond has won a vast amount of money by pinching Kamal's methods of cheating at backgammon. There follows an exciting chase through the crowded and colourful Indian street markets in which the local electric cars (looking rather like golfing trolleys) perform an impressive selection of stunts, jumping over vehicles, driving on two wheels and so on. Once on foot, Bond and his assailants weave their way around men lying on beds of nails or walking over hot coals, sword swallowers and other exotic acts of Indian street life, until 007 shakes them all off.

Gobinda gets his second chance when Bond escapes from Kamal's palace. Kamal organizes an impromptu tiger hunt when he realizes that Bond is missing, and Gobinda and his gang hunt him down in the surrounding jungle. Apart from the hunters, Bond has to contend with spiders, tigers (he orders one to 'sit' – and it does), snakes, leeches and crocodiles. He eventually escapes using jungle creepers, Tarzan-like, to reach a nearby tourist boat.

When Bond is aboard the train taking the circus across the East German border, Gobinda tries again, climbing over carriages and finally pushing Bond off the train (007 survives, rolls down an embankment, picks himself up and begins the long journey to the airforce base on foot).

Left *Gobinda is one of Bond's more menacing protagonists. He is played by Indian actor Kabir Bedi who, among other Hollywood roles, appeared in several episodes of the long-running TV series Dynasty.*

Right *Even three-wheeled vehicles can do astounding tricks when Bond is involved.*

But the climactic fight is on the small plane in which Kamal and Gobinda have kidnapped Octopussy. Bond scrambles on to the tail-fin and, once airborne, Gobinda is ordered outside to sort him out. There follows one of those death-defying stunts that the Bond films are famous for as he and 007 slug it out on top of the plane. Finally, Gobinda falls off, Bond and Octopussy jump to safety and Kamal (who is piloting the plane) crashes into the mountains below.

Above *Octopussy and Bond find they have a lot in common – 007 holds his injured leg up during the traditional clinch with the leading lady at the end of the film.*

Below *One of Bond's more inventive ways of silently moving around in the dead of night!*

The Bond Girl

Octopussy

Maud Adams becomes the only leading female player to appear in two Bond movies when she returns as Octopussy. (Her previous role was as Andrea Anders, Scaramanga's girlfriend in *The Man With the Golden Gun*.) With her bevy of specially trained acrobatic women, Octopussy is the brains behind the jewel-smuggling operation (although she is unaware of Kamal's and Gogol's ulterior motive). She is fabulously wealthy and lives near Udaipur in a palace on a floating island which Bond penetrates disguised as a crocodile. She is known as Octopussy because of her beautiful blue-grey pet octopus which produces a poisoned venom.

Despite being Kamal's accomplice, she does not have his predilection for disposing of 007. Her father, it turns out, was a British major who Bond discovered was corrupt. He faced disgrace and a court-martial when Bond found him out, but was able with Bond's acquiescence to commit suicide

instead. She is grateful to 007 for giving her father an honourable alternative and this immediately creates a bond between them. Octopussy becomes one of the few Bond women to begin her affair with 007 before the dénouement of the film – in fact, she even offers him a job in her organization.

The Victim

Vijay

The Indian tennis star Vijay Amritraj makes his acting debut as Vijay, Bond's Udaipur contact. He introduces himself to Bond at the airport by playing the 'James Bond theme' on his snake-charmer's pipe. His entire role in the film is a series of in-jokes about his tennis playing as he lands a job as a professional at one of Kamal's clubs, disposes of intruders with a well-placed backhand and fights off interlopers with his tennis racquet.

But when Gobinda hires a deadly band of assassins, one of whom wields a circular saw attached like a yo-yo to a string, Vijay meets his untimely end. The band go over to Octopussy's island, attempting to kill Bond; but in the ensuing fight he, of course, proves less easy a target than his Indian friend.

The Background Story

The locations for *Octopussy* took the Bond crew around the world. Among the spectacular locations were: Checkpoint Charlie in Berlin where agent 009 tries to cross to the West; the Nene Valley Railway – a standard-gauge railway running the 8 km (5 miles) between Wansford and Orton Mere, near Peterborough in England where the scenes aboard the circus train were filmed; RAF Upper Heyford which doubled for the US Airforce base in Feldstadt, West Germany; and, of course, Udaipur in India. Permission to film at the various palaces – including the palace of the former rulers of Udaipur which houses magnificent mosaics, inlaid floors and roof gardens – was given by the current Maharaja of Udaipur.

The film's highlights are its dual climaxes, the first of which takes in West Germany. It is a race against time whether Bond can reach the US Airforce base before the atom bomb explodes. When he is thrown off the circus train, he hitches a lift, then steals a car, crashes through the base's barriers and, disguised as a clown, tries to convince the US commander that there really is a bomb in the base of the cannon used for the human cannonball act. Naturally, the commander thinks he is joking and a comic fight develops while Bond convinces everyone that he is serious. Meanwhile, General Orlov has been discovered as a jewel thief (the Soviets deny the atomic bomb incident ever

Above *Tennis star Vijay Amritraj has no need to prove his expertise with a racquet. But as Vijay in the film he finds his backhand serves an unusual purpose.*

Right *James Bond is not clowning about. He is running a desperate race against time to disarm the atomic bomb that Kamal has planted in the US Airforce base in West Germany.*

happened) and is shot by his own side as he is trying to escape to West Germany. Once again, détente is preserved as the main action of the film ends.

But the stars of the film are Octopussy's girls, an army of accomplished acrobats who perform in the circus as well as undertake other duties. They are played by a veritable collection of Bond beauties, headed by Suzanne Dando, the captain of the British women's Olympic Gymnastics team in Moscow. They include: Carole Ashby, an ex-hostess of British TV's *Sale of the Century* quiz show; Carolyn Seaward, a former Miss England and runner-up in the Miss Universe contest; Mary Stavin from Sweden who won the Miss World contest in 1977 and Cherry Gillespie, who plays Octopussy's second lieutenant, a dancer with Pan's People who regularly appeared on British TV's *Top of the Pops*. Two of these girls, who put in a lot of hard work promoting *Octopussy* around the world, were rewarded with parts in the next Bond movie, *A View to a Kill*. Mary Stavin appears in the pre-title sequence and Carole Ashby is a part of the 'butterfly act' at the Eiffel Tower restaurant.

The acrobats contribute an unusual second climax to the film when, led by Octopussy, they attack Kamal's palace to wreak their revenge. The women climb up ropes, scale walls and perform all kinds of tumblers' tricks to overpower his guards and penetrate his stronghold. While they are overwhelming the palace with ease, Octopussy is kidnapped and taken to a waiting plane (on which the death-defying stunts are performed). All's well that ends well, of course, and she retires with Bond to her floating island.

DOSSIER

007 OCTOPUSSY 1983 130 minutes

Producer
Albert R. Broccoli
for Eon Productions

Executive producer
Michael G. Wilson

Director
John Glen

Scriptwriters
George MacDonald Fraser,
Richard Maibaum, Michael G. Wilson

Director of photography
Alan Hume

Production designer
Peter Lamont

Action unit director
Arthur Wooster

Special effects supervisor
John Richardson

Action sequences arrangers
Bob Simmons, Remy Julienne

Supervising editor
John Grover

Main title designer
Maurice Binder

Music
composed and conducted
by John Barry

Song
'All Time High' lyrics by Tim Rice,
sung by Rita Coolidge

Distributor
MGM/United Artists

Cast includes
Roger Moore (James Bond)
Maud Adams (Octopussy)
Louis Jourdan (Kamal Khan)
Kristina Wayborn (Magda)
Kabir Bedi (Gobinda)
Steven Berkoff (General Orlov)
Vijay Amritraj (Vijay)
Robert Brown (M)
Walter Gotell (General Gogol)
Desmond Llewelyn (Q)
Geoffrey Keen (Minister of Defence)
Albert Moses (Sadruddin)
Lois Maxwell (Miss Moneypenny)

Locations
filmed on location in India,
Germany, USA, England
and at Pinewood Studios, England

A VIEW TO A KILL

*Roger Moore's farewell to the Bond series saw him pitting his wits against
a pair of unusual villains – even by 007's standards.*

Ski chases, underwater dramas and underground fights have become the staple diet of the Bond movies, yet each new film manages to maintain the excitement by giving these elements new twists and approaches. *A View to a Kill* is no exception; these devices are all present and fully employed to enhance the dynamics of the plot. There is by now something comfortably reassuring about this formula, and a key factor in the fascination of a new Bond film nowadays is watching how the film-makers will put it into practice this time. Fleming's *From a View to a Kill* (he took the phrase from the third verse of 'D' ye Ken John Peel', a Cumberland hunting song written in 1820) is one of the short stories in his collection *For Your Eyes Only*, but the film is based only loosely on one or two incidents in it.

One of the most effective aspects of *A View to a Kill* is its mingling of two different kinds of humour – the characteristic self-mockery that pervades the later films of the series is coupled with a newer element which verges on slapstick.

The pre-title sequence is, as always, a showcase for the first kind of humour. Like *The Spy Who Loved Me* this sequence relates to the main plot of the film. Among the icy wastes of north-eastern Russia Bond finds the body of another British agent. The Soviets spot him and he has to flee. There follows a spectacular chase – involving skis, snowmobiles and helicopters. Just as Bond seems cornered, the cavalry arrives in the shape of a Union Jack sprouting up from a man-hole cover on an iceberg. It turns out to be the entrance to a British Secret Service boat which carries our hero to safety.

The new humour, on the other hand, is seen at its best in the marvellously drawn cameo of a San Francisco police captain (reminiscent of the character of Sheriff J.W. Pepper in *Live and Let Die* and *The Man With the Golden Gun*) and the car chase in which he is involved. Bond and his girl, Stacey, are trapped in the burning City Hall building. They escape, but only to find themselves under arrest for murder. 'I'm James Bond of the British Secret Service', protests 007. 'Yes, and I'm Dick Tracy', responds the unbelieving copper.

In a city famed for cinematic car chases, the one that follows stands out in its combination of action and humour. Stacey is driving a fire engine while Bond is hanging onto the ladder which is out of control and swinging back and forth across the

street in scenes reminiscent of silent comedy. The climax, in which the fire engine manages to jump a slowly rising bridge, is equally farcical. The police cars are caught – inevitably – on the wrong side of the bridge and slide back down it smashing into each other on the way. As the captain berates his officers for their carelessness, it becomes obvious (at the edge of the screen, behind his back) that his own car is about to disappear beneath a hefty block of falling concrete (actually the counter-weight of the bridge). The whole episode would not have looked out of place in a Keystone Kops adventure.

Above *Bond hangs on for all he is worth as Stacey drives an out-of-control fire engine around the streets of San Francisco.*

Left *May Day (Grace Jones) proves her strength with a stolid KGB agent.*

Below *The sparks are about to fly when the San Francisco police captain finds out that his fleet has been wrecked.*

The Assignment

On the dead body of agent 003 (discovered in the snow and ice) a microchip is found. But this is no ordinary piece of silicon, it is one specially designed by the British to withstand the destructive magnetic pulse that accompanies a nuclear explosion. Agent 003 must have obtained it from the Soviets who, in turn, must have had access to British research. Top of the list of suspects is Max Zorin whose horses continually win races that their pedigree suggests they should not. Bond is sent off to investigate and goes to a horse sale at Zorin's magnificent French château. There he discovers that the horses have microchips implanted in their legs which, when activated by a transistor radio in the riding crop, overcome the horses' fatigue. Bond also discovers that Zorin has another plan for his microchips. He intends to take control of the world market by creating an earthquake along the San Andreas and Hayward faults and thus flooding Silicon Valley, the home of the US microchip industry, killing thousands of scientists and engineers in the process.

Equipment Issued

Most of Bond's equipment is used while he is a guest at Zorin's château. He has a bug detector under the head of an electric razor, a pair of sun-glasses enabling him to see through darkened windows and a tiny camera in his ring to take pictures of the guests. Q's experiment in this film is 'snooper', a small dog-like robotic surveillance machine. Ironically, the only thing it is used to survey is 007 himself – when M sends Q (and snooper) out to track him down at the end of the film.

Above *May Day has to save her skin by parachuting off the Eiffel Tower to avoid being captured by Bond. This famous landmark is one of several stunning real locations which grace the action scenes in* A View to a Kill.

Below *Snooper is a small robot surveillance machine which Q uses to track down his errant agent. It even follows Bond into the shower.*

Below *Zorin (Christopher Walken) gets his kicks from practising judo with his partner-in-crime May Day.*

Enemy Personnel

Max Zorin

According to M, Max Zorin is a leading French industrialist and, on the face of it, a staunch anti-Communist with influential friends in the government. He has accumulated two fortunes – the first in oil and gas, the second in electronics. He is also a successful horse breeder.

But there is more to Zorin than meets the eye. He was born in Dresden and fled from East Germany in the Sixties (with, it later transpires, KGB backing). Now, having double-crossed his Russian masters, he is bent on destroying Silicon Valley and cornering the world microchip market. With his dyed blonde hair and whitened skin, Christopher Walken (who won Best Supporting Actor Oscar for *The Deer Hunter*) plays the part of the psychopathic Zorin with an offhandedness which increases the sense of his maniacal power.

May Day

Zorin's intimate assistant May Day is played by black rock singer Grace Jones, who had made her screen debut shortly before in *Conan the Destroyer*. She is a classic Bond villain who prefers actions to words. In flowing creations by costume designer Emma Porteous, which encase May Day from head to toe, Grace Jones looks and acts like an opponent worthy of Bond's best endeavours.

Her first brush with 007 is at the Eiffel Tower where she kills French agent Monsieur Aubergine with a poisoned dart disguised as a butterfly. She leads Bond on a chase up the tower only to jump off at the top with a black-and-yellow striped parachute (reminding the audience that she is more of a wasp than a butterfly). Bond follows in a stolen taxi which manages to run even when cut in half in a crash. They both end up on a pleasure boat on the River Seine. But where May Day lands on her feet, 007 lands in a wedding cake and loses the game.

May Day teases Bond in this fashion throughout the film only to change sides – as nearly all Bond's conquests eventually do – when she realizes that Zorin has deserted her. Finally, she commits the ultimate sacrifice, blowing herself and the detonator up to save Silicon Valley.

Throughout the film, it gradually becomes apparent that more links Zorin and May Day than mere coincidence of interest. It turns out that they are both the result of a genetic experiment performed in the concentration camps which produced children who all grew up to be highly intelligent and super fit. It also made them psychotic which is, of course, the problem.

Above *May Day saves the day when she drives the detonator out of the Lucky Strike mine to prevent a catastrophic explosion. Unfortunately, she cannot avoid blowing herself up.*

Above right *Stacey (Tanya Roberts) is in a typically tight corner as she tries to escape from Zorin's disused mine before the flood waters catch up with her.*

The Bond Girl

Stacey Sutton

Ex-*Charlie's Angel* Tanya Roberts plays Stacey Sutton, the damsel in distress of this piece. She is first sighted by Bond at Zorin's horse sale, mysteriously arriving and leaving by helicopter. When he turns up later in San Francisco, Bond learns that her father was swindled by Zorin and she is bent on revenge. Stacey spends a large proportion of the film dangling dangerously over various edges – elevator chutes (during the fire at City Hall), underground pits (in Zorin's mine where the explosives are stored to trigger the earthquake) and from the Golden Gate Bridge. This leads to 007's most oft-repeated line of the film – 'Give me your hand, Stacey'. Of course, he gets more than just her hand in the end.

The Victim

Sir Godfrey Tibbett

One of the best characterizations in *A View to a Kill* is Patrick Macnee's Sir Godfrey Tibbett, a racehorse trainer who arranges Bond's invitation to Zorin's sale. He becomes a chauffeur for the occasion and gives a wonderful performance as an upper-class 'gent' imitating a worker. He meets his fate at the hands of May Day, ironically in a car wash – as befits his new status.

Macnee was used to more active roles when he played John Steed in *The Avengers*. (He follows Honor Blackman and Diana Rigg from the TV series into the Bond films while Joanna Lumley went the other way).

Above *Bond never relaxes on the job. Here he is trying to wheedle some information out of an East German spy, Pola Ivanova (Fiona Fullerton).*

Left *In the grounds of the château at Chantilly, Sir Godfrey Tibbett (Patrick Macnee) poses in his guise as a chauffeur in front of his Rolls-Royce. The château was used in the film as the location for Zorin's residence.*

The Background Story

The locations of *A View to a Kill* are stunning even in a series renowned for its visual spectacle. Production designer Peter Lamont makes good use of actual locations like the Eiffel Tower. The location for Zorin's château was Chantilly, a historic and magnificent building with enormous cavernous stables built in 1719, so legend has it, by Louis de Bourbon who was convinced that he would be reincarnated as a horse. The château provides not only an elegant setting for Zorin's guests – and his horses – but also a racecourse. Zorin challenges his adversary, 007, to a bizarre steeplechase in which fences move back and forth, hedges are suddenly raised, bars vary in height from rider to rider and fellow horseracers attack Bond. Not surprisingly, 007 loses the race – and the thoroughbred stallion offered as a prize by Zorin if he can complete the course.

Another startling set for *A View to a Kill* is the disused silver mine which Zorin is filling with explosives in order to set off the double earthquake which will destroy Silicon Valley. The large stage at Pinewood Studios had been burnt down shortly before – during the shoot of *Legend*. It had to be rebuilt before this new set could be constructed.

The new stage was named the 'Albert R. Broccoli 007 Stage' by studio head Cyril Howard as a thank-you to Broccoli for the work he had brought over the years to the studio and the British film industry as a whole. The stage was dedicated during a snow storm on a freezing cold day but nevertheless numerous members of the press turned up as a tribute to the Bond series' producer.

The mine chamber, complete with streams, bridges, rolling stock, wooden office sheds and a veritable maze of tunnels and shafts, has the makeshift feel of a building site which adds to the tension as Stacey and 007, joining forces with May Day, race against time to defuse the detonator and stop the explosion.

After May Day blows the detonator up – and herself with it – Zorin escapes, with Stacey in tow, by means of his Portakabin which transforms itself into an airship with a cunning design that would do justice to Q's imagination. Bond, who is hanging from the ship by a thread, ties it up to the suspen-

> The Amberley Chalk Pits Museum, a collection of local machines and tools in the south of England, complete with a narrow-gauge railway, appropriate rolling stock and tunnel entrance, became the location for the disused silver mine. However, the interiors of the mine were constructed on the 007 stage at Pinewood.

sion cables of the Golden Gate Bridge. Zorin and Bond face their final showdown from the dizzy heights. It is a scene only made possible by the help of the San Francisco Fire Department and the directors of the bridge. It is a breathtaking sequence with everybody involved – not just Stacey – losing their grip as Bond and Zorin battle it out. But even a super-intelligent, genetic freak is, in the end, no match for the top agent of the British Secret Service.

The scenes in San Francisco could not have happened without the co-operation of Mayor Diane Feinstein. To show their appreciation, the producers decided to hold the film *première* in San Francisco with the proceeds – over $75,000 (then around £50,000) – going to a charity of the mayor's choice: the Mayor's Youth Fund. The cheque was presented to the mayor on the esplanade outside the Palace of Fine Arts by a man in a black suit who parachuted from a helicopter in true 007 style.

Zorin's airship becomes entangled with the girders of the Golden Gate bridge in San Francisco. In the ensuing fight, everyone has trouble holding on to something solid.

DOSSIER

007 A VIEW TO A KILL 1985 131 minutes

Producers
Albert R. Broccoli, Michael G. Wilson for Eon Productions

Director
John Glen

Scriptwriters
Richard Maibaum, Michael G. Wilson

Director of photography
Alan Hume

Production designer
Peter Lamont

Action unit director
Arthur Wooster

Ski director and camera
Willy Bogner

Special effects supervisor
John Richardson

Action sequences arrangers
Martin Grace, Remy Julienne

Editor
Peter Davies

Main title designer
Maurice Binder

Music
composed and conducted by John Barry

Title song
lyrics and performed by Duran Duran

Distributor
MGM/United Artists

Cast includes
Roger Moore (James Bond)
Christopher Walken (Max Zorin)
Tanya Roberts (Stacey Sutton)
Grace Jones (May Day)
Patrick Macnee (Tibbett)
Patrick Bauchau (Scarpine)
David Yip (Chuck Lee)
Fiona Fullerton (Pola Ivanova)
Desmond Llewelyn (Q)
Robert Brown (M)
Walter Gotell (General Gogol)
Lois Maxwell (Miss Moneypenny)
Geoffrey Keen (Minister of Defence)

Locations
filmed on location in France, USA, Iceland, Switzerland, England and at Pinewood Studios, England

THE LIVING DAYLIGHTS

The introductory film for Timothy Dalton, the fourth actor to star as 007.
With locations as richly diverse as Gibraltar, Vienna, Morocco and the Austrian alps,
plus a quite exceptional cast, this promises to be one of the best Bonds yet.

The fifteenth James Bond 007 film produced by Eon Productions is based on a short story by Fleming which was first printed in the *Sunday Times* and then published as part of the *Octopussy* book. Scripted by Richard Maibaum and co-producer Michael G. Wilson, *The Living Daylights* once again brings together the talents that helped make the previous Bond movies so successful – John Glen remains in the director's chair; Peter Lamont continues as production designer and John Richardson is in charge of special effects for the third time.

But there is, of course, a new element to the team as Timothy Dalton takes over the mantle of 007. Dalton, a Shakespearian actor of repute, brings to his Bond characterization a whole new dimension. He sees the world-famous agent as a man who lives his life in the fast lane so that he is always on the edge with deadly encounters never too far away.

On the screen his powerful presence makes him immediately identifiable as James Bond – so much so that the pre-title sequence is able to take liberties with his introduction to the audience. Three of M's top double-0 agents are on a training exercise – to penetrate Gibraltar's defence system with the crack troops of the SAS trying to prevent them. The agents parachute down on to the famous rock and as the action unfolds, the audience soon discovers which is Bond, even without a proper introduction.

He becomes embroiled in an exciting chase in which he is hanging on to the top of a Land Rover racing along the precarious slopes of the rock's summit. Finally the vehicle goes over the edge, plumetting into the depths below and taking the agent with it. A split second before the Land Rover explodes in a mass of flames, the agent escapes and parachutes to safety, landing on the canopy of a luxurious yacht where a typical Bond beauty is sunning herself.

Left *Timothy Dalton, who makes his debut as 007 in* The Living Daylights, *brings a dangerous edge to the character.*

Below *A typical breathtaking Bond stunt occurs in the pre-title sequence when the three double-0 agents make a jump from a Hercules aircraft to land on Gibraltar. Their instructions are to attempt to penetrate the Rock's radar installation to test its vulnerability.*

Above *A daring escape – Bond style – occurs in the pre-title sequence when the Land Rover being driven by a KGB assassin crashes over the edge of the Rock of Gibraltar with 007 hanging precariously to its top. As the Land Rover explodes, Bond falls free, with the flames threatening to engulf him.*

Below *An artist's rendering showing some unusual optional extras on 007's new Aston Martin 'Volante'. In* The Living Daylights *this extraordinary vehicle proves a worthy successor to Bond's previous gadget-packed cars – the Aston Martin DB5 first seen in* Goldfinger *and the Lotus Esprit which made its debut in* The Spy Who Loved Me.

The Assignment

A high-level KGB agent, General Koskov, has defected to the West from Bratislava. His escape plans are nearly ruined when a female sniper attempts to shoot him. (Bond, whose job it clearly is to stop the sniper, does not strictly follow orders and aims to maim rather than kill.) At his debriefing, Koskov tells of the existence of operation *'Smiert Spionen'* which translated from Russian means 'Death to Spies'. The plan includes a death list, through which, Koskov claims, General Pushkin (General Gogol's replacement as head of the Soviet Secret Service) intends to eliminate the best British and American agents. The West will retaliate, he reasons, leading to a full-scale war in which the Soviets will come out on top.

Before Koskov can release more details of the plan, however, he is supposedly recaptured by the KGB in a daring ruse which involves a terrorist disguising himself as the milkman to penetrate the safe house where Koskov has been taken. While M believes that Bond's refusal to kill the sniper who fired at Koskov makes him unable to be impartial, Bond is the only person with a real lead and he sets off for Czechoslovakia to trace the sniper.

Equipment Issued

The Living Daylights sees the return of Bond's Aston Martin – but the DB5 of *Goldfinger, Thunderball* and *On Her Majesty's Secret Service* has now been updated to the 'Volante' model. Equipped with an array of devices including laser-beam cutters, automatic missiles, rockets, a head-up display (as seen in a

Bullet-proof glass

Hinged number plate

Rocket jet propulsion unit

Head-up display

Laser beam cutter

Automatic missiles

B549 WUU

Studded tyres

Automatically protruding skis from sills

Below *In Blayden House, Koskov (Jeroen Krabbé, standing) is explaining the 'Smiert Spionen' plan to M (Robert Brown, right), Bond and the Minister of Defence. He is revealing to the assembled company the alleged Soviet death list – which he smuggled out in his shoe – of British and American spies.*

Above *Q (Desmond Llewelyn), Bond and Miss Moneypenny (Caroline Bliss) discuss the qualities of the ghetto blaster as a weapon in Q's workshop.*

cockpit), studded tyres and protruding skis for driving on ice, it is one of the most adaptable of Bond's cars to date and he puts it to good use in several awkward situations.

Q's standard-issue vehicles, however, are two Audis: a 200 Quattro driven by Bond in Bratislava, and a 200 Avant which 007 uses in Tangier in his surveillance of General Pushkin.

In addition, Bond has a key-ring, specially made for the film by Philips – the kind that responds when you whistle for it. Q demonstrates some of its tricks. Whistle 'Rule Britannia' and it emits a stun gas with a range of 1.5 m (5 ft). It is also densely packed with explosives – and, to trigger the detonation, what more appropriate for Bond than a wolf whistle?

There is, of course, the traditional humorous scene in Q's laboratory where a range of new devices is being perfected. One of the highlights of the filming period was the visit of the Prince and Princess of Wales to the set at Pinewood Studios where the royal couple were introduced to Q's den. They saw a radio which fires explosives – literally a ghetto blaster – being demonstrated and the princess tried out a prop bottle (made of sugar glass) by smashing it over her husband's head.

Princess Diana snatches a rare opportunity to knock 'The Living Daylights' out of Prince Charles with a prop bottle (made of sugar glass) when the royal couple visited the Bond sets at Pinewood Studios on 11 December, 1986. In the background is actor Jeroen Krabbé (partially hidden, right), who plays Koskov.

Right *In Kamran Shah's Afghan mountain headquarters Bond and Kara Milovy (Maryam d'Abo) discover that their perilous adventures together have aroused feelings much deeper than they had realized.*

Below *Having the front nearside wheel blasted off the Aston Martin 'Volante' by the police does not hinder Bond and Kara's escape plans. With the aid of a rocket motor, ski outriggers and a 45-degree incline the Aston Martin becomes airborne, astonishing the Czech border patrol guards.*

The Bond Girl

Kara Milovy

Kara is a young cellist whom Bond first sees playing in an orchestra in Bratislava. Later, Bond and Kara's paths cross again, and it becomes clear that she is, in fact, a friend of Koskov's. But is she just a friend or is she a KGB agent or someone even more sinister? It is Bond's mission to find out – which he does in typical fashion, breaking Kara into the West and showing her a good time as only he knows how.

Maryam d'Abo who plays Kara is not the traditional glamour girl of previous Bond movies. Although very beautiful, she does not wear much make-up nor elaborate hair styles. She is more natural-looking and, as such, becomes the ideal complement for a very Eighties James Bond. Although she was brought up and educated in Paris and Geneva, Maryam was born in England of a Dutch father and Georgian mother. English is her second language and she speaks it perfectly without a trace of an accent. She has appeared in a number of TV series and films but her part in *The Living Daylights* will undoubtedly push her into the international limelight.

Above *Kara playing the Stradivarius cello named the 'Lady Rose', in the Schlosstheater in Vienna. Although the cello was a present from Koskov, the bullet hole will be a constant reminder of her escapades with Bond.*

Enemy and Other Personnel

Whitaker

Whitaker is a tough wheeler-dealer who climbed to the top of his trade – arms dealing – by his own efforts. His home in Tangier contains several militaria exhibits which give clues to his personality – he has lifelike waxwork models in his own image of many infamous ruthless leaders from Genghis Khan to Adolf Hitler and has several scale models of renowned battles complete with regiments of miniature lead soldiers from which he studies the tactics and strategy of war.

Whitaker (Joe Don Baker), a self-styled general with his own army, prepares for his final showdown with Bond. He is defending his 'territory' with a super-rapid-fire machine-gun with a specially designed bullet-proof upper body shield. But it takes more than high-tech gimmickry to stop 007.

Whitaker is played by American actor Joe Don Baker who made a name for himself as a tough hero in the Seventies with films such as *Guns of the Magnificent Seven*, *Junior Bonner*, *Charley Varrick* and *The Pack*. More recently he appeared as a baseball player alongside Robert Redford in *The Natural* and delighted English audiences with his role as a CIA agent in the television series *Edge of Darkness*.

Whitaker is clearly the brains behind the 'Smiert Spionen' operation and is using it for his own ends which involve complicated diamond and opium deals. But who is his Soviet contact? While Koskov claims that Pushkin is running the Moscow end of the plot, Pushkin claims that Koskov is the villain. It is left to 007 to untangle the problem.

Kamran Shah

Art Malik, who shot to fame in the award-winning British TV series *The Jewel in the Crown*, plays Kamran Shah, the leader of the group of Afghan freedom-fighters, who comes to 007's aid after Bond has befriended him. He followed *The Jewel in the Crown* with a major part as the excitable solicitor in David Lean's production of E.M. Forster's novel, *A Passage to India*.

General Koskov

Leading Dutch actor Jeroen Krabbé plays the Soviet defector, KGB General Koskov, who becomes the central figure in a deadly game of intrigue and double-dealing. One of Holland's most popular actors, Krabbé has had his own chat show on Dutch television, a music programme on radio, and has regularly appeared on TV in a variety of drama productions. He is also established as a professional painter. His film career includes appearing with Glenda Jackson and Ben Kingsley in the British-made *Turtle Diary*. In America he recently completed *Jumping Jack Flash* with Whoopi Goldberg and co-starred with Richard Gere and Kim Basinger in *No Mercy*, for which he received rave notices.

General Pushkin

Versatile Welsh actor John Rhys-Davies plays the role of General Pushkin, Head of the KGB. General Gogol, played by Walter Gotell, who held this post in previous Bond movies, has been promoted to the foreign service. John Rhys-Davies has not only worked extensively with the Royal Shakespeare Company but also has many leading roles on British TV to his credit – including *The Sweeney*, *I Claudius* and *The Naked Civil Servant*. His international feature films include starring roles in *Raiders of the Lost Ark*, *Victor/Victoria* and *Shadow of Kilimanjaro*, among others.

General Pushkin (John Rhys-Davies) confronts Whitaker at his home in Tangier. Whitaker's megalomania can be deduced from his waxwork models of history's ruthless leaders whose faces have all been cast in his own image.

Above *In order to enter Blayden House, the high-security hide-out to which M has taken Koskov for debriefing, Necros (Andreas Wisniewski) disguises himself as the milkman. He incapacitates the chef (Michael Percival) with his favourite weapon – the headphone cord of his Philips personal stereo.*

Below *After Bond and Kara are captured by General Koskov, they are taken to Afghanistan. There 007 befriends Kamran Shah (Art Malik), the leader of a group of Afghan freedom-fighters, by helping him escape from his Soviet jailers.*

In return Shah assists Bond by attacking a Russian military airport, enabling 007 and Kara to commandeer the Soviet transport plane in which they hope to fly to safety. Kamran Shah (centre) and his forces create havoc at the airport with grenades, machine-guns and rifles.

Necros

The first villain encountered in *The Living Daylights* is Necros, a terrorist who is clearly indispensable to Whitaker since he has a talent for disguise and mimicry. He can, in fact, seemingly effortlessly merge into any scenario. It was Necros who captured Koskov from the safe house, first by disguising himself as a milkman and then by imitating the plummy accents of the butler to gain further admittance. He is a ruthless killer whose favourite trick is to use the headphone leads of his Philips personal stereo to garrotte his victims.

Necros is played by Andreas Wisniewski, a 1.8 m (6 ft 2 in) dancer with a Polish father and German mother. He has appeared recently in a number of pop promos, one of which (directed by Ken Russell) led to a part in his first English-language feature, *Gothic*. In *The Living Daylights* he joins the ranks of some of the most memorable Bond villains.

Saunders

Head of Section V, Vienna, Saunders is an integral part of the story, as he is the agent who is contacted by Koskov about his defection. Thomas Wheatley, who appeared as the registrar in the recent British TV series *The Singing Detective*, plays Saunders as an officious, somewhat pompous, functionary. However, when the chips are down he comes through for Bond in true Secret Service style.

Right *At a public gathering at the Trade Centre in Tangier, it appears as if Bond has shot General Pushkin, the head of the KGB. In the ensuing chaos, Bond has to make his escape from the police across the rooftops of the* casbah — *during which he makes use of the local resources by stringing an Eastern carpet between two telegraph poles and riding it daringly to safety.*

Below *Landing from his 'magic carpet' ride, 007 surprises a local tradesman (played by Eddie Kidd, the well-known British stuntman) by leaping onto the back of his moving motorcycle.*

Above *A murderous imposter is trying to wreck the Secret Service defence exercise in Gibraltar. Bond finds himself desperately hanging on as the KGB assassin skilfully drives his Land Rover along the winding roads that lead to the Rock's summit, trying to throw off 007.*

The Background Story

The Living Daylights, like the previous Bond movies, delights in exotic locales for its action. The pre-title sequence was shot in Gibraltar, the tiny rocky British dependancy on the southernmost tip of Spain. To film the perilous Land Rover ride and its fall over a 90 m (300 ft) cliff, the permission of the MOD had to be sought. The stretch of road that was used is so dangerous that, under normal circumstances, a special driving test is insisted on for those negotiating its twists and turns. It makes a spectacular location for a gripping and unusual car chase.

After Gibraltar, the film crew moved to Morocco where they filmed in Tangier and Ouarzazate. In Tangier, the Bond team took over the *casbah* for several days to film an imaginative chase sequence in which Bond escapes from his pursuers by means of a Moroccan carpet and telegraph wires while the desert town of Ouarzazate stood in for Afghanistan where Bond becomes entangled with rebels while investigating 'Smiert Spionen'.

Once again, *The Living Daylights* manages to com-

bine the essential ingredients of Bond in a new and vibrant way, giving fresh magic moments which may last as long as some of the memorable scenes of the past: Honey Ryder first emerging scantily clad from the water in *Dr No*; Bond ejecting his stupified passenger from the Aston Martin DB5 in *Goldfinger*; 007 skiing off the edge of the mammoth precipice (and surviving) in *The Spy Who Loved Me*. But this Bond movie also marks the debut appearance of Timothy Dalton in the central role of 007. This debut could well be a momentous chapter in the history of the Bond series when another book is written one day titled: *The Official James Bond 007 Movie Book – The Second Twenty-five Years*.

DOSSIER

007 THE LIVING DAYLIGHTS   1987

Producers
Albert R. Broccoli, Michael G. Wilson
for Eon Productions

Director
John Glen

Associate producers
Tom Pevsner, Barbara Broccoli

Scriptwriters
Richard Maibaum, Michael G. Wilson

Director of photography
Alec Mills

Production designer
Peter Lamont

Action unit director
Arthur Wooster

Special effects supervisor
John Richardson

Action sequences arrangers
Paul Weston, Remy Julienne,
B. J. Worth

Editors
John Grover, Peter Davies

Main title designer
Maurice Binder

Music
composed and conducted
by John Barry

Title song
Performed by a-ha

Locations
filmed on location in Morocco,
Gibraltar, Austria, England, USA
and at Pinewood Studios, England

Cast includes
Timothy Dalton (James Bond)
Maryam d'Abo (Kara Milovy)
Joe Don Baker (Whitaker)
Art Malik (Kamran Shah)
John Rhys-Davies (General Pushkin)
Jeroen Krabbé (General Koskov)
Andreas Wisniewski (Necros)
Thomas Wheatley (Saunders)
Desmond Llewelyn (Q)
Robert Brown (M)
Caroline Bliss (Miss Moneypenny)
Geoffrey Keen (Minister of Defence)
Walter Gotell (General Gogol)
John Terry (Felix Leiter)
Julie T. Wallace (Rosika)
John Bowe (Feyador)
Nadim Sawalha (police captain)

Distributor MGM/UA
A United Artists picture

Index

Figures in italics refer to captions; headings in inverted commas indicate characters in the films. Entries in the dossiers which appear at the end of each chapter are not included in the index.

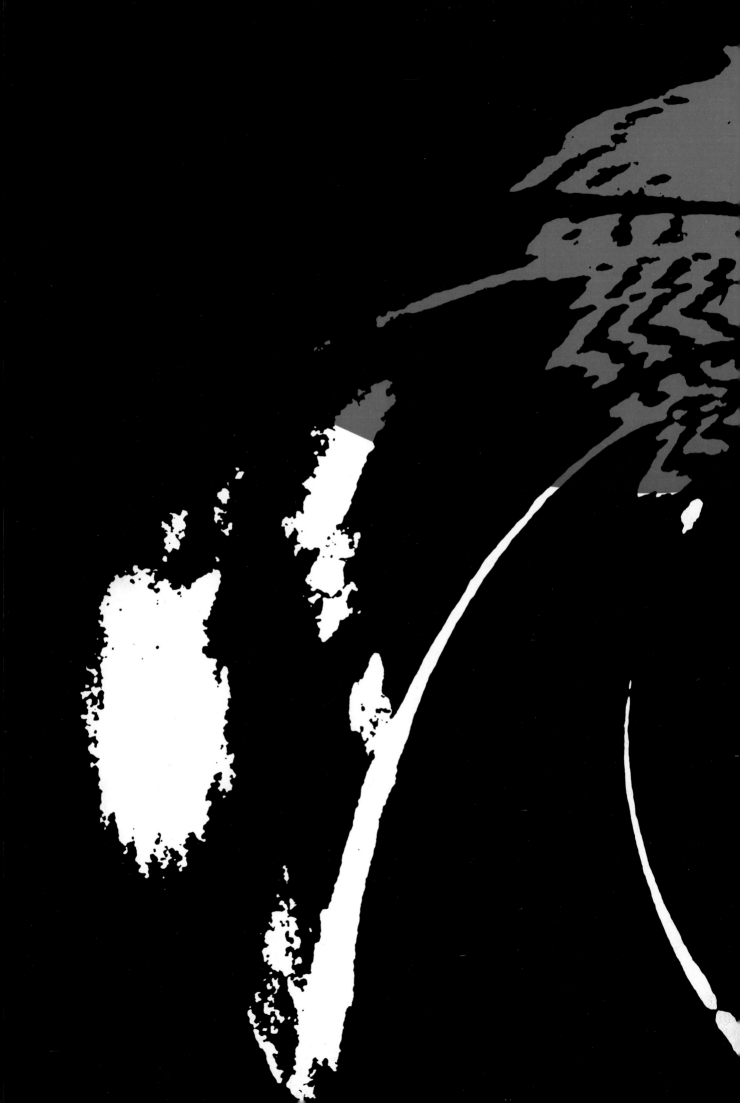